the
Rainbow
of renewal

D1352876

Dedicated to
Benjamin Muhalya
inspiring friend
true African
faithful servant of Christ

the
Rainbow
of renewal

Daily Bible reflections for Lent and Easter

Michael Mitton

Text copyright © Michael Mitton 2005
The author asserts the moral right
to be identified as the author of this work

Published by
The Bible Reading Fellowship
First Floor, Elsfield Hall
15–17 Elsfield Way, Oxford OX2 8FG
Website: www.brf.org.uk

ISBN 1 84101 436 2
First published 2005
10 9 8 7 6 5 4 3 2 1 0
All rights reserved

Acknowledgments
Unless otherwise stated, scripture quotations are taken from The New Revised
Standard Version of the Bible, Anglicized Edition, copyright © 1989, 1995 by the
Division of Christian Education of the National Council of the Churches of Christ
in the USA, and are used by permission. All rights reserved.

A catalogue record for this book is available from the British Library

Printed in Singapore by Craft Print International Ltd

Contents

Foreword

You have to be very world-weary not to be touched by the sight of a rainbow. I still dash straight outside at the rumour of one, standing in the rain and searching the sky for a glimpse of it. But I have never read a book about rainbows before.

Like puppies, flowers and still mountain lakes, rainbows suffer badly at the hands of the sentimental. Real rainbows appear at the meeting of highly volatile natural elements—heat and cold, sun and rain, storm and calm. In fact, that is the reason we see them at all. They trace the vulnerable, fragile frontier between hope and threat—lit by fierce shafts of sun against a background of dark thunderclouds. That is the sign of a rainbow. In the Bible, it is a sign of hope that appears in places that are otherwise turbulent and uncertain.

This is a book about renewal, but the term 'renewal' is easily misused. The very gift that is intended to open up life to radical, new possibilities and the glorious vision of God becomes monochrome. It is all too easily narrowed to certain experiences, phrases and ways of behaving.

Through imaginative reflection, Bible reading and prayer on each of the colours of the rainbow, Michael Mitton guides us into an exploration of the whole width of human life and experience, and reflects on what faith might mean in those places. The joy and the light are here, but there is also pain and darkness. They must all find their place in God's enduring and transforming love. That is what real renewal means, and only *real* renewal can help us in the increasingly uncertain weather of our times.

There is a poem I know that asks what Christian ministers are for and what they do. One answer comes back: they try 'to colour in God'. Michael Mitton is someone whose friendship and writing have always added colour to my own relationship with God. This book is a rich and wise contemplation of the myriad colours of our own lives as they are stirred and awakened in the renewing gift of the Spirit.

According to the old folk stories, there is a crock of gold at the end of a rainbow. Well, there are riches throughout this rainbow of a book. It is a gift for all who long to know life and God in full colour.

David Runcorn

Introduction

For most of my Christian life, I have cherished the theme of renewal. I was baptized at a few weeks old, and nourished on a diet of Anglican Book of Common Prayer worship. It did not mean a great deal to me until the Holy Spirit started to stir my soul in my teenage years and influences such as Billy Graham made their mark on me. As a 19-year-old, I had an overwhelming experience of the Holy Spirit at a tiny Pentecostal church on a cold February morning. It was an experience that brought life to every aspect of my faith, and contributed to me offering myself for the ordained ministry. Serving in charismatic churches, I discovered how a church community could share in the experience of renewal. For eight years, I worked as Director of Anglican Renewal Ministries; during this time, I encountered many inspiring individuals and churches across the world that testified to the renewing work of God's Spirit. I also began to see how transformed individuals and transformed churches could be used by the Spirit to transform the communities where they served.

Though my work was primarily concerned with charismatic renewal, I loved the contact I made with many other expressions of the renewing work of the Spirit in the Church and the world. One particularly enjoyable task was being asked to edit *The Way of Renewal*, a report published by the Board of Mission of the Church of England General Synod in 1998.[1] This gave me the opportunity to cover a very wide range of renewal experiences and showed the diversity of the Spirit's renewing work. I write this book as the Project Officer for Renewing Ministry in Derby Diocese, and my work includes rejoicing with those who are witnessing renewal, and supporting those who pray for it and long for it. Renewal does not belong to a particular section of the Church—it is intrinsic to the work of the Spirit, and the Spirit is available to all churches.

The Rainbow of Renewal has been written as a Lent book, for Lent is a very good time to take a step back and make space for God to do his renewing work. Traditionally, Lent has been connected with Jesus' journey into the wilderness, from which he returned in the power of the Spirit to begin his ministry in Galilee. We too have the opportunity to be led by the Spirit into a desert place, a place of vulnerability and dependence on God, a place of repentance and resistance to evil; from such a place we too can return to our Galilees in the power of the Spirit.

The best way of using this book would be to start on Ash Wednesday with the first reading and work your way through to Easter Day. All the readings have a connection with the broad theme of renewal. The last two weeks have a closer link to the Easter story, and the last week in particular focuses on the great events of cross and resurrection. If you therefore get behind in your reading, you may want to jump to Week 7 when you reach Holy Week, as these readings will be of help as you prepare for Easter.

The book will also work well if you read it outside Lent. It will provide you with readings for six-and-a-half weeks, or you may like to spend more than one day with an individual theme if it particularly appeals to you. The last thing you want is to be driven by a sense of guilt, feeling you must do your reading every day! Just raise your sail to catch the wind of the Spirit and ask God to use this book to lead you on a personal journey of renewal.

The structure of each day is as follows:

1. *Scripture passage:* you may want to look up this passage in your Bible and check its context. Sometimes I will be referring to what comes before or after the given passage.
2. *Comment:* I have written a comment (not a detailed commentary) on the passage, which may include some information to help you understand it better. My main focus is drawing out what this passage is saying about the theme of renewal.
3. *Reflection:* there are one or two simple questions to guide your thoughts after you come to the end of the reading. You may find

these helpful, or you may prefer to let your own questions emerge while you are reading and reflect on those.

4. *Prayer:* again, this is available for you to use if it's helpful, or you may prefer to say your own.

Meeting in a group

You may like to use this book for group study. You could meet once a week, after you have completed each week's readings, and share what you have been learning. You might find it helpful to keep notes of your thoughts. The questions for reflection at the end of the day's reading will help you form your response to each theme.

The following questions are suggested to help you structure the group meeting:

1. Which of the readings has meant most to you? Share what God has been saying to you. Give each person in the group space and opportunity to share their experience.
2. Have you found anything difficult to understand? Others can share their insights to help clarify.
3. Is there something you would like to do in response to what you are learning, personally, in your church, at work, or in your community?

The rainbow

At first, I could not think of a title for this book, but then the idea of the rainbow came to mind. The rainbow has seven colours, and so I have given one to each week-long section. At the beginning of each week, I provide a short introduction, which includes an explanation of why I have used the particular colour for the theme. These themes are not the only ones to do with renewal, but I wanted to focus on seven that I feel are particularly relevant for today. As you work your way through this book, I hope you will discover more and more about the multi-coloured love of God that arches over our lives, always full of promise, and always drawing us into new life.

Dedication

I have dedicated this book to the Revd Benjamin Muhalya. I made friends with Benjamin when we were both students at St John's College, Nottingham, in the 1970s. It was he who first opened my heart to his homeland. I visited Kenya just before I was ordained, and spent time with him and his family in their home town of Nakuru. Ten years ago, I visited Kenya again and spent more happy days with Benjamin, who by then was serving in Eldama Ravine.

As I was writing this book, I heard news from his daughter, Margaret, that Benjamin had become seriously ill, and not long after I had completed the last chapter, Margaret phoned me from Nairobi to say that her father had died.

I have no idea how old Ben was, but I know that he served as an Anglican priest for around 30 years. He was a man of gentle spirit and evangelistic fire, and I have always admired him greatly. I suspect his humility did not allow him to see what a great gift he had been, not only to the church in Kenya, but to people like myself in other parts of the world. If the world was full of Benjamins, it would be a most beautiful place of many rainbows.

Mourning (Violet)

Introduction

Our daily readings begin on Ash Wednesday, the first day of Lent. Many churches that use liturgical colours will be removing the various bits and pieces of green linen, and replacing them with purple, the colour that is associated with mourning, because Lent is traditionally a time of sorrow and fasting. A world that is obsessed with pleasure-seeking of many kinds is somewhat puzzled by a group of people opting for six weeks of apparent misery. It wasn't that long ago that it was the accepted custom to give up things during Lent. In my home, it was sweets and chocolates. The state of my teeth bears testimony to the important role sweets and chocolates played in my childhood, and to be denied these for a wearisome six weeks (apart from the blessed 'Refreshment Sunday' in the middle of Lent) was a very real cause for mourning. Somehow, as children, we never argued with it—it was just part of life. Everyone else seemed to do the same, and my father assured us that it was good for our character, and it would make Easter that much more special if we had courageously held out for the six weeks of Lent—and my, the chocolate Easter egg did taste good!

I sometimes wonder whether Lent meant more to my parents and their generation because of what they experienced during the Second World War. In the days of rationing, they knew what it was to do without so much of what I took for granted. Furthermore, they had a strong sense of both personal and corporate grief. I have not yet heard of a family who lived through those years without being touched by deep grief in one way or another. My parents were grateful that no close relatives were killed during the war, but they would often speak of much-loved friends who had died. My grandmother's best friend was Mrs Potts. She had two sons, whom both my parents adored—they were closest friends. It was a grim day when the news came that both boys had been killed in action on the same day. Some years later, I was born and they chose to name me after one of those sons, Micky. There was a sense that placing the name in a new life helped in the process of mourning and moving on.

Lent is a season that takes us into the theme of mourning. It takes us with Jesus into the wilderness, where we are invited to reflect on our lives and give up those things that lead us away from God. As Lent moves on, so our focus moves increasingly to the passion of our Lord Jesus, and we journey with him to the cross, until we gather with the women and John at the foot of the cross and grieve. For many of us, the Good Friday devotional service is a special time of becoming aware of the old, old story again; we remind ourselves that we had a part to play in Jesus' suffering, and that it is by *his* stripes that we are healed.

Any mourning story will inevitably connect us with other mourning experiences we have known in life. It may be personal, or, as it was for my parents' generation during the war, it may well have a corporate dimension. In these first days of Lent, we are going to look at this theme of mourning in more detail, and use as our guide Bible passages in which the community of God's people shared in a corporate experience of mourning. As we look at these passages, we will see that renewal often begins with mourning; it is not a mourning without hope, but neither is it a mourning without pain.

Exiles in Babylon

By the rivers of Babylon—there we sat down and there we wept when we remembered Zion. On the willows there we hung up our harps. For there our captors asked us for songs, and our tormentors asked for mirth, saying, 'Sing us one of the songs of Zion!' How could we sing the Lord's song in a foreign land? If I forget you, O Jerusalem, let my right hand wither! Let my tongue cling to the roof of my mouth, if I do not remember you, if I do not set Jerusalem above my highest joy. Remember, O Lord, against the Edomites the day of Jerusalem's fall, how they said, 'Tear it down! Tear it down! Down to its foundations!' O daughter Babylon, you devastator! Happy shall they be who pay you back what you have done to us! Happy shall they be who take your little ones and dash them against the rock!

PSALM 137

This psalm gives us an insight into a most devastating experience of corporate grief. When Joshua triumphantly marched the faithful people of God into the promised land, the future looked wonderful. God had rescued his people from Egypt; he had led them through the wilderness, and they then enjoyed an era of occupying the land that had been promised to them right at the beginning of their story of faith (Genesis 12:7). In time, God granted them their wish of having a king, and Saul was the one chosen for the task.

However, it was not long before Saul's descendants erred and strayed into just about every type of offence imaginable, and the kingdom became increasingly vulnerable to foreign invaders, as God withdrew his protection from the rebellious people. Eventually the unthinkable happened: a foreign people invaded Jerusalem; the mighty temple, which looked so indestructible, was pulled down; the king was blinded and led pathetically to imprisonment, and much of the population was marched ignominiously out of the city on another desert walk, this time not to the Holy Land, but away from it to Babylon.

So it was that they found themselves as refugees in a foreign land, where nothing was familiar, their faith was disregarded, and they were treated like slaves. Worst of all, God seemed to have abandoned them. They had believed he would preserve Jerusalem no matter what, and yet when it came to the crunch, he was apparently nowhere to be seen.

Thus, a group of them find themselves slumped down by the waters of Babylon, and all they can do is to think back to the good old days of Zion. Babylon was very different to Judea: it had an intricate system of canals, running across a huge, flat plain, which would have felt so different to the hills and valleys of Judea. They sit down by one of these canals and chat together, and one of them might say, 'Do you remember how at this time of year, we would go up to the temple to make our offering, go through that mighty gate and hear the sound of the busy market, and listen to the prayers of the priest…' Others may join in, until it becomes too painful to continue. Each time they remember, they weep. It is what grieving people do. Those who have lost people they love want to recall many memories. We say, 'Do you remember how he used to…', 'Do you remember she loved to…', and it is a sort of bitter-sweet experience. We feel comforted by the remembrance, and yet it often brings tears, as we are aware of the extent of our loss.

The people of God in Babylon are no longer able to sing, and so they hang up their lyres. How painful it must have been when the captors taunted them, saying, 'Go on, sing us one of those odd songs you used to sing back in Jerusalem.' These were songs full of meaning and emotion for the Judeans, but for the Babylonians they were a source of mockery.

But the psalm tells us that these people of God, though deeply grieving, had an impressive stubbornness. Their inability to sing in a strange land does not mean they will forget Jerusalem—far from it. They may not understand, but they will hang on to hope. They'd sooner lose their hands and their tongues than forget Jerusalem. The psalm ends with terrible words that we find almost impossible to read—the vengeful killing of innocent children makes us think of the callous terrorist blasts that are all too familiar in our day. There is deep hatred of the perpetrators of exile here, and the mourners give themselves strength in the only way they know how, which is to spit out venomous threats at their captors.

I have no idea what it must be like to be led away from a home and people I love and be taken to a land where all the customs and cultures are quite alien to me, where I cannot communicate because I don't know the language, and the people among whom I live view me with suspicion and distaste. I am all too aware that in this often sad and violent world that experience is far too common, and the issue of asylum seekers in 21st-century Britain is alerting us to the problems and pains of refugees. But for most of us this kind of exile is not something we are likely to experience personally. Nonetheless, it is quite possible to know a very deep sense of corporate loss at a way of life that once we took for granted, but now seems a million miles away.

The film adaptation of the first book of *The Lord of the Rings* begins with a mysterious voice narrating the words: 'The world has changed. I feel it in the water; I feel it in the earth; I smell it in the air. Much that once was is lost, for none now live who remember it.' The rest of the dramatic story builds upon the fact that things have taken place that have deeply disturbed the world, and no one really understands or remembers how it was, or how we got to this point. There are many in our churches who may feel this way: 'The church has changed... much that once was is lost.' There are people in the church where I serve who have been part of the congregation all their lives. They are in their 70s and 80s, and they have seen many different phases in the life of the church. They readily look back at the days when the building was full, the choir-stalls full of enthusiastic choristers of all ages, the Sunday School thriving, and the takings at the parish bazaar enough to cover the church costs. Now they look round at a society that has all but turned its back on God; they see that few churches have their own clergy, but have to share them with other churches; they witness clergy ignoring so many of the traditions that were once hallowed. Much that once was is lost. By the waters of the 21st-century post-modern, texting, Big-Brother-watching, eBay-shopping world, they sit down and weep.

Of course, it is not just the elderly who have this experience. Any of us can drive around this land and see once large churches in urban and rural situations now struggling with dwindling congregations, battling with the ever-increasing financial burdens of leaking roofs and crumbling walls, and we too can find ourselves thinking back to the good old days when churches looked very successful. We too can feel the dull ache of despair afflicting our souls.

And yet, paradoxically, this experience can be the beginning of renewal. For the people described in the psalm, their response was anger against the perpetrators of the humiliation and destruction that they had suffered. Today, in our longing for renewal, we can also easily end up with a 'blame' mentality, so that we look for those whom we can hold responsible for getting us into this situation. Others during that time of exile would have just shrugged their shoulders and said in effect, 'Oh well, this is now how it is. Let's settle down here in Babylon.' But thankfully there were prophets around who gave an inspiring lead to help people move from despair to hope and, in time, to make a journey of renewal to build a new Jerusalem. We shall look at this a bit more tomorrow, but today's task is to acknowledge how we feel about the losses that we have experienced individually and corporately in connection with the life of the church. You may be part of a church that once was alive in many ways, but now things have gone quiet and dry; you may once have belonged to a church that seemed so alive, but where you are now feels as if it lacks life by comparison; you may have left your church because you were disappointed with it, and now you live your Christian life more or less alone. Or maybe it is not your personal experience that bothers you, but you have a sense of connection with the wider community of the Church, and you grieve because in some areas of its life it has experienced many losses. If, on the other hand, you are in a church that is ablaze with renewal, then give thanks to God (and say a prayer for those who envy what you have).

Reflection

Think about your church situation—is it one of renewal at the moment? If it is, where do you see the renewal expressing itself? If not, what are your feelings about its situation? What is in your heart as you reflect on this? Grief? Blaming? Reluctant acceptance? Longing for the old days? Hope? You might like to try writing a psalm to express your feelings, making it your prayer to God.

Prayer

Lord, today is the beginning of Lent, and I choose to journey with you in these coming days. Only you know where you will lead me. Give me all that I need to let go of all that would weigh me down, and to be open to the new things you want to show me. Lead me by the waters of renewal.

Thursday

Suffered Hope

For thus says the Lord: Your hurt is incurable, your wound is grievous. There is no one to uphold your cause, no medicine for your wound, no healing for you. All your lovers have forgotten you; they care nothing for you; for I have dealt you the blow of an enemy, the punishment of a merciless foe, because your guilt is great, because your sins are so numerous. Why do you cry out over your hurt? Your pain is incurable. Because your guilt is great, because your sins are so numerous, I have done these things to you. Therefore all who devour you shall be devoured, and all your foes, every one of them, shall go into captivity; those who plunder you shall be plundered, and all who prey on you I will make a prey. For I will restore health to you, and your wounds I will heal, says the Lord, because they have called you an outcast: 'It is Zion; no one cares for her!'

JEREMIAH 30:12–17

At a young age, Jeremiah heard God calling him to a very difficult and demanding ministry. He was to be a prophet at a time of enormous upheaval, as he would witness the destruction of Jerusalem under King Nebuchadnezzar. The Lord warned him not to marry or have children, because the imminent sweeping judgments would make life for the next generation utterly precarious (Jeremiah 16:1–4). He was a vulnerable man, given to fears and dreads, yet he remained totally committed to his call, and persistently and faithfully declared God's word to a people who were determined not to listen. Almost certainly, he witnessed firsthand the full horror of the destruction of Jerusalem in 587BC. He watched the last king in Jerusalem, Zedekiah, being led captive out of the city. Zedekiah had to witness the horrifying sight of his sons being murdered before him. It was the last thing he was to see on earth, as he was then cruelly blinded by his captors. For a time, Jeremiah stayed in Jerusalem with Gedaliah, whom Nebuchadnezzar had made governor of the fallen city. There was always a threat that he too would be taken off to Babylon, so it was not long before he left for the relative safety of Egypt when he must have been around 70 years old. It is believed that he died there, far away from his beloved homeland.

Jeremiah has rather a reputation for being an old misery. Certainly, quite a lot of his writing makes for pretty grim reading. But there again, he was writing at a time when everything was collapsing around him, and the world as he and everyone knew it was coming to an end. Because he listened to God and observed his society so closely, he could see the death of the culture and its traditions long before it happened. He watched the known world disintegrate, and he felt its pain deeply. He was no dispassionate prophet standing on the sidelines, lobbing prophecies in every now and again just to rub salt into the wound. He wrote out of his own personal agony ('My anguish, my anguish! I writhe in pain! Oh, the walls of my heart!' Jeremiah 4:19). What hurt him so deeply was the failure of his contemporaries to listen to what was going on, but stronger even than his love for his fellow humans was his love for God. He adored God, and felt God's pain over a people who time and time again spurned his love because they thought they knew better. Jeremiah therefore took upon himself grief both on earth and in heaven.

He not only writes to express the pain, however. He is also a writer of great hope. The theologian Walter Brueggemann calls him the 'voice of suffered hope', and our passage today is one that expresses both the grieving and the hope. Chapters 29 and 30 of the book of Jeremiah contain much material about hope; it's quite a relief to get to it after 28 chapters about pain! Our passage starts with a statement that seems to be entirely lacking in hope: 'Your hurt is incurable.' The situation is entirely hopeless. What the people desire so much is not going to happen. They want all the horror of invasion, destruction and exile to go away; they want the dark clouds to blow over and everything to return to peace and quiet again. Jeremiah, who has listened to God deeply, reports that there is no medicine that can cure the sickness, no lover who will offer care. The people's behaviour has been so terrible that the only way forward is the judgment of God. Then, in the middle of this passage, there is a very surprising word. It is in verse 16, and it is the word 'therefore'. When Jeremiah's listeners heard that word 'therefore' they would have feared the worst—they would have anticipated further words of judgment. However, this 'therefore' leads not to more words of judgment on the people of God, but to words of protection and care. God will rise up in judgment on their enemies. He will send *them* into exile; *they* will be plundered; *they* will suffer.

What we see in these verses is the utter depth of God's commitment to his people. The passage starts with the facts: the people have carried out every crime possible; they have poisoned themselves and made themselves terminally ill; the situation seems beyond redemption. Therefore, God will act. Yes, he will let them face the consequences of their actions, but he's not going to leave them to their own devices. He's going to roll his sleeves up, come down and transform even the most desperate of situations. It's an extraordinary 'therefore'. It's as if God is saying, 'Your offences are so great, therefore I will reveal the great depth of my love.' While the passage starts with the obvious (that they are beyond healing), after the 'therefore', the words of hope come: 'I will restore health to you, and your wounds I will heal' (v. 17). And there is another stated reason here as to why God should act so generously. It is 'because they have called you an outcast...' (v. 17). God will not have his enemies mocking his people. He is like a protective parent rushing into the playground and challenging the bully. Yes, his child may have misbehaved, but he will be the one to do the disciplining, not some abusive stranger. Only he can discipline with divine love.

This passage speaks to a people who are in mourning and shock. It speaks also to those who feel that they have really messed up their lives through what they have said or done. It is a passage that pre-empts the great act of grace, in the coming of God to our world in the person of Jesus.

Reflection

Are there situations in your life where you feel you have messed up? Maybe you feel God is standing there with a kind of 'I told you so' kind of look on his face. Have a look at this passage again, and dwell especially on the promise: 'For I will restore health to you, and your wounds I will heal, says the Lord'. What might this promise mean to you in your situation?

Prayer

Lord, you are a holy God and your ways are perfect. I am far from perfect, and I live in a society that has abandoned so many of your ways. You must feel sad and angered by the many things we do which spoil what you have planned for us. Please forgive me, and help me to hear your divine 'Therefore…'. Come with healing, and let me hear your voice so that, like Jeremiah, I may speak your words of comfort and challenge to others.

Letting Go

As he was setting out on a journey, a man ran up and knelt before him, and asked him, 'Good Teacher, what must I do to inherit eternal life?'

Jesus said to him, 'Why do you call me good? No one is good but God alone. You know the commandments: "You shall not murder; You shall not commit adultery; You shall not steal; You shall not bear false witness; You shall not defraud; Honour your father and mother."' He said to him, 'Teacher, I have kept all these since my youth.'

Jesus, looking at him, loved him and said, 'You lack one thing; go, sell what you own, and give the money to the poor, and you will have treasure in heaven; then come, follow me.' When he heard this, he was shocked and went away grieving, for he had many possessions.

MARK 10:17–31

You can't help feeling a bit sorry for this young man. He seems to get so much right, and yet he receives an incredibly hard request from Jesus. He asks a fairly good and spiritual question, 'What must I do to inherit eternal life?' If I had been there at the time, I imagine I would be thinking that Jesus would have been very pleased with that question. I would have expected him to have said, 'Repent and believe and be baptized,' or something like that. Rather than commending him for a good gospel question, however, he seems to be extraordinarily picky about the words the man uses in his question. 'Why do you call me good?' says Jesus. I would have been thinking, 'That's not important, Lord. It was probably just a way of being polite and respectful', and I think I would have felt a bit irritated with Jesus for effectively putting this man down, and certainly putting him off. Before we know where we are, Jesus is quoting the commandments at him. This is not an evangelistic technique that I instinctively warm to! It doesn't completely put the man off, though, and he rather impressively tells Jesus that he has kept all these commandments since he was young.

Then Mark, who is telling us this story, mentions one very special fact: 'Jesus, looking at him, loved him.' Whatever Jesus says from now onwards, it is said with the voice not of reprimand, nor of cajoling to do better. It is said with the voice of love. I wonder how Mark knew that Jesus loved the man at that point. Whoever it was who first witnessed this incident and reported it to Mark, they noticed something very loving about Jesus' disposition towards this young man.

So what does Jesus say in response to this good young man who has kept all the commandments since his youth? He says, 'You lack one thing.' For a moment, those witnessing this encounter might have said, 'Hardly—look how wealthy he is. He's not short of anything!' But, according to Jesus, he lacks something, and the only way to gain it is to give everything away. If he gives away all his earthly treasure, he will gain heavenly treasure. There then follows a moment of great sadness. Don't forget that Jesus loved this man, and as he looked deeply into his soul, he saw that the only way he could gain his greatest desire was by giving away the possessions that he valued so highly. There was no compromise route. If the man kept his wealth, he would always value that more highly—he was too devoted to it. The man was also very sad. Jesus asked of him the one thing that he felt unable to do—part with his treasured wealth. So he goes away grieving.

Jesus is teaching his disciples through this encounter. He is introducing them to a very basic principle of life, that sometimes to gain what is really valuable, we have to let go of what is really of less value. It is often to that less valuable thing that we attach great importance, and feel pain if there should be a separation. The immediate context of the incident is material wealth, but by the end, Jesus makes it clear that whatever we give up for the sake of the kingdom of God will ultimately be returned to us many times over. And some of this giving up is so hard—it's actually impossible. Then Jesus adds that nothing is impossible with God.

The young man in this story goes off grieving, which is ironic because Jesus is actually calling him to engage in a proper grieving —a letting go that will bring new life. Over the centuries, many have known a deep liberation in giving up material wealth for the sake of the kingdom of God. Francis of Assisi is one such example. The implications of this story are wider than material wealth, however. There can be all sorts of things to which we are so attached that we fail to enter into a different kind of wealth that God wants to give us.

Personal and church renewal often starts with us being willing to let go of something that we once valued. In the life of the local church, it may be the 'way we have always done it'. It may be the willingness to let go of a style of worship that we have long cherished, but which has become an object of our devotion in its own right and keeps us from engaging with the new experiences to which God wants to lead us. It may be forms and styles of renewal that meant so much to us only a few years ago, but which don't have much effect now. If we really want renewal in our personal and corporate church life, then we must allow Jesus to come to us, to look on us and love us, and say to us, 'You lack one thing. Go and let go of…' And we may say, 'Oh no, Lord, not that. That's impossible.' Before we run away, we need to wait to hear those words, 'For God all things are possible.'

Reflection

In what ways do you desire renewal in your life and in the life of your church? See if you can be specific. Spend some time in quiet; listen to your own heart and to God to see if there is anything you need to let go in order to move on into the new life that God has for you.

Prayer

Lord Jesus, you know my heart better than I. Look on me with your deep love, and help me to discover anything that would prevent me from receiving your new life.

Saying Farewell

'Therefore be alert, remembering that for three years I did not cease night or day to warn everyone with tears. And now I commend you to God and to the message of his grace, a message that is able to build you up and to give you the inheritance among all who are sanctified. I coveted no one's silver or gold or clothing. You know for yourselves that I worked with my own hands to support myself and my companions. In all this I have given you an example that by such work we must support the weak, remembering the words of the Lord Jesus, for he himself said, "It is more blessed to give than to receive."'

When he had finished speaking, he knelt down with them all and prayed. There was much weeping among them all; they embraced Paul and kissed him, grieving especially because of what he had said, that they would not see him again. Then they brought him to the ship.

ACTS 20:31–38

We come today to a very touching passage about the apostle Paul. He is busy on one of his missionary journeys and has been evangelizing and planting churches in Macedonia and Greece. Luke is the writer of this story; he was also part of this adventure, as he writes of the things 'we' did. He tells us that Paul is in a hurry to reach Jerusalem, to get there for Pentecost (Acts 20:16), and so will not have time to look in on the church at Ephesus. The leaders at Ephesus are keen to see Paul, however, and so they come to him when he is at Miletus, just a few miles down the coast. There is quite a sense of sorrow and foreboding at this meeting. As he speaks with the elders, he summarizes some of his ministry (vv. 18–21), reminding them of how he preached the gospel to Jews and Gentiles alike. No doubt, as he tells them this, there is further sharing of news about how the gospel is spreading in Ephesus and the regions beyond.

Paul then relates how the Spirit is compelling him to go to Jerusalem, and how the Spirit has on several occasions made it clear that when he gets there prison and hardships await him. Thus, he says (v. 25) that he won't see them again, and gives them a final charge, part of which is in today's reading. It must have been a rather shocked and sorry group of leaders who listened to Paul. He is keen that they remember him as one who worked hard and honestly among them, for he suspects that when he gets to Jerusalem, he will face an unfair trial with all kinds of lies told about him. He wants these friends to remember the truth, and not be swayed by rumours that may wind their way round Asia Minor following his arrest. I suppose you could argue that this suggests Paul is rather more interested in his personal reputation than he should be, but I think he is concerned for the reputation of all those who have been entrusted with the work of bearing the gospel. It is interesting that even in these early days of church life, Paul guards himself against accusations of financial mismanagement. It's as though he can see what a problem this will be to the church in the generations after him.

So, after giving his charge, Paul kneels down with them all and prays. There is something very moving about this scene. They all undoubtedly hold Paul in very high regard—here is this remarkable soldier of Christ who is sailing around the Roman world fearlessly proclaiming the gospel. He has been used by God to deliver people from evil, and to heal the sick. Many miracles have been performed by him, and only a few days before, he has actually been used by the Lord to raise back to life a young man, who had died after falling from a window (admittedly due to nodding off during Paul's preaching, which was a little less complimentary! See Acts 20:9).

Paul is a great man by any reckoning, but here he is among a group of friends whom he clearly loves very much, and he vulnerably kneels with them and prays for them. We are then told by Luke that there is a spontaneous outburst of love and grief as the Ephesians bid farewell to him with hugs and kisses. It must be a very emotional scene as Paul boards that ship and sails off to what they all imagine will be a destination of conflict, imprisonment and quite possibly death. In fact, it seems that Paul did manage to visit Ephesus again (1 Timothy 1:3), but clearly the long-range forecast was right, and the day would come when Paul would die an untimely death as a martyr.

I am so pleased that Luke chose to include this story of human warmth and grieving in his book. He might have wanted to focus solely on the many stories of powerful encounters and dramatic preaching, but he chose to include these kinds of rather incidental human stories as well. He did so to help us understand that our faith is not divorced from all the normal human experiences of life.

The gospel had brought about a new level of relationships, in which a travelling messenger like Paul developed deep friendships relatively quickly. Many people, when they first become Christians, are delighted to discover that they become part of a community whose members are willing to talk at a more personal level than often experienced elsewhere in life. This takes them into friendships where there is a depth of prayer and sharing. One of the things I have loved about travelling abroad is meeting other Christians as I find myself forming close bonds with people I have only just met, who are part of a different nation and culture. Despite our different backgrounds, the Holy Spirit is at work among us, enabling us to 'cross borders' and discover our common ground in Jesus. I know a little of what Paul must have felt, because working together for the gospel, even for a short time, can bring about such a depth of friendship that parting can feel like a real grief.

Some people are fortunate because life's circumstances mean that they remain settled in a community and church for many years and seldom have to say 'goodbyes'. Others have known the pain of moving away from friends and family, however, and experience a very real time of mourning. Although this can be painful, sometimes the Holy Spirit can come into our place of vulnerability and help us to become open to a new understanding of God, of scripture and of prayer. We don't lose our sorrow about what we have lost, but it is as if we have made space to embrace something new. It can be a process that takes a while, but it invariably happens. Few of us would choose to say farewell to friends we love and cherish, but in the workings of the kingdom of God, it is reassuring to know that any death has the potential of resurrection that brings about a renewal in our lives.

Reflection

Think of a time when you had to say goodbye to someone you loved, rather as the Ephesian Christians had to say goodbye to Paul. As you reflect on that, can you see ways in which God provided comfort and support? Did the experience help you to become open to whatever new things God was giving you?

Prayer

Lord, thank you for all those who are, and who have been, my friends. Each one has enriched me and helped me on this journey of life. Come with healing where I still carry grief over friends lost, and help me to trust your resurrection power to bring new life in and through my farewells.

Uncertainty (Indigo)

Introduction

Renewal inevitably brings change, and change can bring renewal. If we want to be spiritually renewed, therefore, we will need to be prepared to change. It may not be a change we desire, or a change that we will find comfortable. It is also true that any changes we experience in life can provide opportunities for personal renewal. All changes in life bring losses and gains, and change is particularly painful if what we are losing is something we have greatly cherished. In a time of change, we are nearly always uncertain as to what the gains might be, and we wonder if the gains are going to outweigh the losses. Take moving house, for example: people can decide to move into a bigger and better house, but in the time of the move they can go through real heartache as they become aware of how fond they were of the old house, and feel unsure about a house they have not yet got to know. But in time, they get to know the new one just as well. Life feels exciting and full of promise, and gradually they can let go of the attachment to the old house and fully settle into the new.

This week, we shall be looking at the theme of renewal and change and the consequent feelings of uncertainty that often accompany the experience of change. Indigo strikes me as being a colour that is neither one thing nor the other. I look hard at it and at one moment it looks blue, then at another it looks purple, and I can't quite make it out. It's as though it is not quite sure which colour it is! There's a bit of me that wants to push it one way or the other, but then I slow down and look at it carefully and realize what a very beautiful colour it is. There is something instinctive in our humanity that can feel very uncomfortable with change and uncertainty. We can feel rather vulnerable and we can long for a quick transition to something sure and secure. Times of uncertainty, however, are part of life, and as we shall see through our readings this week, they can be occasions that, like the colour indigo, are full of creative beauty.

Moving On

When the horses of Pharaoh with his chariots and his chariot drivers went into the sea, the Lord brought back the waters of the sea upon them; but the Israelites walked through the sea on dry ground. Then the prophet Miriam, Aaron's sister, took a tambourine in her hand; and all the women went out after her with tambourines and with dancing. And Miriam sang to them: 'Sing to the Lord, for he has triumphed gloriously; horse and rider he has thrown into the sea.' Then Moses ordered Israel to set out from the Red Sea, and they went into the wilderness of Shur. They went for three days in the wilderness and found no water. When they came to Marah, they could not drink the water of Marah because it was bitter. That is why it was called Marah. And the people complained against Moses, saying, 'What shall we drink?' He cried out to the Lord; and the Lord showed him a piece of wood; he threw it into the water, and the water became sweet. There the Lord made for them a statute and an ordinance and there he put them to the test. He said, 'If you will listen carefully to the voice of the Lord your God, and do what is right in his sight, and give heed to his commandments and keep all his statutes, I will not bring upon you any of the diseases that I brought upon the Egyptians; for I am the Lord who heals you.'

EXODUS 15:19–26

It is impossible to imagine what it must have felt like. The children of Israel had known years of abuse at the hands of the Egyptians. Now, as they watch the waters of the Red Sea engulf the very people who had made their lives such a misery, they know they are free. They are moving into a completely new world. Not surprising, then, that Miriam gets her tambourine, gathers the other women, and they sing and dance and celebrate a new dawn. Only three days later, however, the people are not happy. They are desperately thirsty. This new world, which looked so good one day, now seems not a lot better than the old one. Although it offers them water, it is bitter, and the people look around the wilderness and begin their complaints. In response, Moses performs a wonderful miracle and assures them that the Lord will be their healer. If you read on, you will find it is not long before they are complaining again, and the complaints roll on as they travel deep into the desert on their way to the Promised Land. As it turns out, their time of uncertainty lasts forty years, which is a very long time to be in a time of transition. They had hoped that the change would be easy—one day slave, next day free. But life is rarely as simple as that.

For the Israelites, the world they were leaving was one they were delighted to put behind them. There are times in our lives, though, when we are forced to move on from a world with which we were quite at ease, and we find ourselves in a wilderness of uncertainty as we await the new. Theologian, priest and anthropologist Gerald Arbuckle has written a book called *Grieving for Change*, which emphasizes the need to grieve the old properly if we are to embrace the new. Quoting the Latin poet Ovid, who wrote 'suppressed grief suffocates', he starts his book with a story from his childhood in the 1940s:

As a little boy of nine, I would deliver newspapers daily to subscribers in my small village in New Zealand. Each day I would meet an elderly Christian Maori Chief, who would be standing silently before a tribal meeting house faced with wooden carvings depicting his ancestors and the former greatness of his culture of pre-colonial days. He would break from his contemplation to greet me warmly but gently.

I looked forward each day to that smile and being treated as though I were an elder myself. Only later did I realize the source of his warmth and why he would stand before the carvings every day. He was grieving over the loss of the identity and sense of belonging to his people. Yet as he pondered this loss, sometimes even in tears, a new life would take hold of him. He would identify the sufferings of his people with those of Christ and believe that through the Saviour's resurrection he and his tribe would discover a new heart, a new strength. New leaders would emerge to evoke a revitalised sense of tribal self-worth through ways radically different from those of their ancestors. He did not know when this would happen. But the more he acknowledged the death of the old, the more he hoped.[2]

This Maori chief was engaging in a most therapeutic piece of theology. He was owning the grief of losing a culture that had meant so much to him and his ancestors. He took the pain of this to the cross of Christ, and like a priest he also took the suffering of his people to the cross, for he knew that here was the place where grieving could be transformed into resurrection hope.

Renewal usually involves some kind of motion. We are required to make a journey. In the case of the people of Israel, it was a welcome journey away from a land they hated. In the case of the Maori chief, it was a journey away from a world that he and his people loved. Both groups had to leave; both groups found themselves in a time of uncertainty. But it was a time of uncertainty that was full of possibilities. The people of Israel discovered the law, among other things, during their wilderness period. The Maori chief was discovering a way of integrating his experience into the death and resurrection of Jesus. We cannot hurry such times. They can feel disturbing, but they are often seasons of surprising creativity.

Reflection

Is there anything or anyone you have had to leave recently? Think about how you have journeyed from that former experience into a new experience. How has God led you during this time? What do you need most during a time of uncertainty?

Prayer

God of my ancestors, you have led us and those before us through good times and bad. As a shepherd, you have cared for your flock. Forgive our complaints, and help us to journey as a people of faith.

Time to Change

Samuel took a phial of oil and poured it on his [Saul's] head, and kissed him; he said, 'The Lord has anointed you ruler over his people Israel. You shall reign over the people of the Lord and you will save them from the hand of their enemies all around. Now this shall be the sign to you that the Lord has anointed you ruler over his heritage. When you depart from me today you will meet two men by Rachel's tomb in the territory of Benjamin at Zelzah; they will say to you, "The donkeys that you went to seek are found, and now your father has stopped worrying about them and is worrying about you, saying: What shall I do about my son?" Then you shall go on from there further and come to the oak of Tabor; three men going up to God at Bethel will meet you there, one carrying three kids, another carrying three loaves of bread, and another carrying a skin of wine. They will greet you and give you two loaves of bread, which you shall accept from them. After that you shall come to Gibeath-elohim, at the place where the Philistine garrison is; there, as you come to the town, you will meet a band of prophets coming down from the shrine with harp, tambourine, flute, and lyre playing in front of them; they will be in a prophetic frenzy. Then the spirit of the Lord will possess you, and you will be in a prophetic frenzy along with them and be turned into a different person. Now when these signs meet you, do whatever you see fit to do, for God is with you.'

1 SAMUEL 10:1–7

Today's rather strange passage takes us into the world of the first kings of Israel. Samuel was called to be a prophet of the Lord when he was a child (1 Samuel 3), and throughout his life he gives crucial spiritual leadership to the people of God. When they demand to have a king, it is Samuel's task to discern whom the Lord is calling, and so every day he keeps his ears and eyes open, waiting for God's revelation. One day, the Lord speaks to Samuel and says: 'Tomorrow about this time I will send to you a man from the land of Benjamin, and you shall anoint him to be ruler over my people Israel' (1 Samuel 9:16). On the next day, Samuel is obviously full of expectation. Saul is in the neighbourhood, because he is out looking for his father's donkeys, which have gone astray. The moment Samuel sees Saul, God speaks to him again, making it clear that this young man is to be the king. The good news for Saul is that the donkeys have been found; the bad news is that he is to be the first king of Israel, and nothing in his wildest imaginings could have prepared him for this task.

Our Bible reading starts with Samuel anointing Saul. When he has done so, he delivers a rather involved prophecy about three meetings: two men near Rachel's tomb, who will report to him his father's concern about his long absence; three men going to worship at Bethel, who will give him two loaves of bread; and finally a band of prophets on the way back from the shrine, who will be in a prophetic frenzy. If Saul hadn't any concerns about this king business before, I'm sure he would have had them now. But the situation gets even more bizarre for Saul, because Samuel tells him that he too will go into a prophetic frenzy. Not only that but he will be 'turned into a different person'; I wonder what Saul made of that! I must admit that on a bad day, or at times when I am particularly irritated at my forgetfulness and foolishness, the idea of becoming someone else is really quite attractive. For most of the time, though, I'm happy to be me, with the proviso that much could be improved. But would I really want to become a different person? No, I don't think so. I think that in Saul's case, he didn't have a complete personality change. What I understand Samuel to mean is that in his radically different role as king, Saul would be given a whole range of new gifts from God to equip him, and that these would make him feel quite different.

Any experience of renewal is likely to change us. I imagine that most of us hope that renewal doesn't lead us to become frenzied prophets, and I think it is safe to assume that Saul's situation was rather unusual. People do have real anxieties about spiritual renewal, however. They see, read and hear things about charismatic (or Pentecostal) renewal, and worry that they will have to engage in all sorts of strange activities. I remember the first time that I went to a Pentecostal church. I was 19 years old and knew very little that was outside traditional Church of England practice, but I had read a magazine article about Pentecostals. For some odd reason, I imagined that Pentecostals flew in their meetings, and I was really nervous about this, because if they started flying when I was there, I would quickly be exposed as a non-flying, unspiritual person, deserving of great disapproval. I was not at all reassured when the pastor announced the first hymn and said, 'We shall stay in our seats until verse three, when we shall leave them.' Great was my relief when I discovered that 'leaving seats' meant no more than standing up. As it happens, the service then turned out to be one of great personal renewal for me, where I encountered the Holy Spirit in a most loving and powerful way.

The fact is that any encounter with God is likely to have its effect on our life in some way. It is therefore very normal to carry round inside us some uncertainty about renewal. If I pray for God to renew my faith and my Christian life, how will it change me? If I ask someone to pray for me, will something happen that will be out of my control? Will I weep, laugh, shake, fall and do some of those curious things reported concerning charismatic meetings? I'm sure Saul must have had these anxieties as Samuel slapped him on the back and wished him well as he went on his way. I don't suppose he minded the word of concern from his father and the two loaves of bread. But frenzied prophesying? That must have worried him a bit.

Then Samuel makes one more statement at the end of our passage: 'Do whatever you see fit to do, for God is with you.' Saul will not be at the mercy of some divine force driving him into wild prophecies and ecstatic dancing. He has choice. His renewal is not about being out of control. Moreover, there is great safety here as well: 'God is with you.' This message is given so often to God's people when they are anxious or disturbed. Immanuel, God-with-us, is around. Does that make it safe? Well, I don't think it guarantees a quiet life, but it does mean that the infinite love of God is far closer than we can possibly imagine, and if we can grasp even a little of what that means, we are on a journey of renewal.

Reflection

As God offers his renewal to you, what would you like changed in your life more than anything else? Give a few moments to listen to your longings, and then try and see if you can hear God communicating his response to your request.

Prayer

Spirit of the living God, fall afresh on me.

Listening to the Disturbance

The words of Nehemiah son of Hacaliah. In the month of Chislev, in the twentieth year, while I was in Susa the capital, one of my brothers, Hanani, came with certain men from Judah; and I asked them about the Jews that survived, those who had escaped the captivity, and about Jerusalem. They replied, 'The survivors there in the province who escaped captivity are in great trouble and shame; the wall of Jerusalem is broken down, and its gates have been destroyed by fire.' When I heard these words I sat down and wept, and mourned for days, fasting and praying before the God of heaven.
NEHEMIAH 1:1–4

We return today to the theme of the exile. We join Nehemiah who is living in Susa, which was the major city of Elam (a country east of Babylonia), and it is the winter of 446BC. It is a long time since the destruction of Jerusalem in 587BC, and no one is alive who remembers how it was. Nehemiah will have heard the story time and time again, and he will know that God's people once lived in a far-off, fertile land, a land promised to them by God, a land given by God and won by brave warriors, but a land lost because of faithlessness and foolishness. He has grown up in the land of Elam, and perhaps his family have lived there for more than one generation. For many of them, it feels like home, and they have settled down and made the best of a bad job. Indeed, Nehemiah has not done too badly—he is the cupbearer of the king. Scholars believe the cupbearer was the one who had to choose and taste the wine, and also had to ensure that it was not poisoned. So the job carried some risk! But it also meant that the king had complete confidence in him, and Nehemiah must have earned this confidence through years of faithful service.

I imagine that Nehemiah had been relatively content with his life for many years, until that winter's day when his brother Hanani comes to see him. Hanani has been in Judah with a few friends, and he tells Nehemiah about what he found there. 'How are they doing these days?' asks Nehemiah. Hanani leaves him in no doubt that matters are not good: 'Those who have survived are in real trouble. The walls that used to protect the city have been completely broken down and the once mighty gates have been burnt to the ground.' We don't know if this was the first time that Nehemiah has been touched by the situation in Jerusalem, but now he is certainly affected. We are told that when he hears his brother's report, he sits down and weeps, mourning deeply for his home city and the people who are so vulnerable there. In his deep grief, he cries out to God for help.

The rest of chapter 1 is Nehemiah's prayer, and it is a most wonderful prayer of humility and faith. He prays a prayer of confession on behalf of himself and his family. He is well aware of the sins that led the people of Israel into their sad exile, and with penitence and a sense of urgent petition he calls out to God to use him to bring some kind of healing and restoration to this situation. The rest of the book of Nehemiah is God's answer to this prayer, as God leads his servant to be at the forefront of the rebuilding of Jerusalem.

Moments of real disturbance and uncertainty can unexpectedly visit us, as they did Nehemiah. We can be going along in life quite happily, when something happens that stops us in our tracks and gets us thinking. It might be an unwelcome event, like an illness or loss of job. It might be something good, like falling in love or witnessing a friend come to faith. Or it might be, as it was with Nehemiah, that some issue suddenly comes into sharp focus. For a long time we have kept it at arm's length, but now, all at once, it becomes real. I know of a couple who were settling happily into a leisurely life of retirement, when suddenly, out of the blue, they felt God calling them to assist with a small missionary work in Kenya. Over the next few years, they made a number of visits there, staying for several months at a time and helping to build a support centre for a local community. They had always had a love in their hearts for the poor of the developing world. But one day that love was suddenly quickened and became a call.

Usually, there is quite a time of disturbance and uncertainty between the call and the outworking of the call. In chapter 2:1 of his book, we learn that Nehemiah was serving the king in the month of Nisan, which is the following spring. The king notices his sadness of heart. Nehemiah has tried to keep his inner disturbance to himself, but now it is showing through his service, and the king can see that something's wrong. It is the king's kind concern which allows Nehemiah to tell him why he is so disturbed, and after that it is not long before Nehemiah is saddling up and starting his journey to Jerusalem. Such moments of disturbance and uncertainty are not comfortable, but they can be moments that renew our relationship with God. As with Nehemiah, we are thrown to our knees; our prayers are focused and our hearing sharp; we become open to the miraculous intervention of God, and energized by the surprising ways in which God might lead us. It is not a comfortable time, but it can be full of life.

Reflection

Spend a few moments of quiet reflection and listen to your inner self. Is there anything you are disturbed about? Might God be calling you to make some response to a particular need in your home, church, work, community, or in the wider world?

Prayer

Lord, Nehemiah heard a story of suffering, and his heart was restless until he could respond. Give me an open heart today; help me to risk being touched and disturbed; make me available to hear your call and give me the courage that I will need to follow you faithfully.

Moments of Doubt

When John [the Baptist] heard in prison what the Messiah was doing, he sent word by his disciples and said to him, 'Are you the one who is to come, or are we to wait for another?' Jesus answered them, 'Go and tell John what you hear and see: the blind receive their sight, the lame walk, the lepers are cleansed, the deaf hear, the dead are raised, and the poor have good news brought to them. And blessed is anyone who takes no offence at me.'

MATTHEW 11:2–6

I find this passage very reassuring. In Matthew's Gospel, we meet John the Baptist, whom Matthew introduces as someone who came preaching in the desert (3:1); his message was clear, uncompromising and unequivocal: 'Repent, for the kingdom of heaven has come near' (3:2). Matthew describes this wild man, who is like one of the ancient prophets. He went about in a camel-hair shirt, which must have been extremely itchy in a hot desert, and would have made him look very at home among the wild animals. He lived on a diet of locusts and wild honey. How did he catch the locusts? Did he put the honey on shrubs and branches so the locusts would stick to them? Some wonder if the word for locust actually refers to an edible desert plant. Either way, the diet was fairly basic. I do wonder at John's lifestyle, which was a million miles away from the way we live in 21st-century Britain, where honeyed locusts is just about the only food you don't find on the supermarket shelf!

John seemed so very other-worldly. I don't imagine that he would have been someone whom you could tease about his camel-hair shirt or latest locust recipe. He seemed far too serious for that, and certainly Matthew's description of him is fearsome. As soon as people met him, they wanted to confess their sins, and the poor old Pharisees and Sadducees, those pillars of a respectable religious society, were shouted at by John and told that they were a brood of vipers (3:7). John's confidence about his role as the forerunner of the Christ is so impressive. He gave up everything to lead this penitential and prophetic lifestyle in the wilderness, and there is no doubt that he was a wonderfully effective herald for the coming of the Messiah.

When Jesus was baptized by John (3:13), John's heralding ministry was over. It would have been nice for John if he could have packed up his camel-hair shirt and returned to a more normal life. In today's reading, however, we hear the news that he is in prison. He has openly criticized Herod for taking his brother's wife as his own (14:3–4), and would no doubt have known the huge risk he was taking in doing this. It reveals John's depth of passion for God and his ways of holiness and right living. We might imagine that in prison John would be sitting there singing his psalms, encouraging his fellow prisoners, hearing with delight the stories of Jesus' ministry. But this is where we would be wrong.

For all his confidence and faith, John now appears to be going through a time of deep questioning. In the confines of his prison, he begins to wonder if Jesus really is the Messiah. He hears a few stories, perhaps one story about Jesus appearing to let a woman off for a crime of adultery. Was Jesus going soft? Was he challenging Herod's immorality sufficiently? Whatever the specific causes, at some stage in his lonely imprisonment, John encounters some most unwelcome pockets of doubts.

He has got some good friends who visit him, though, and they must have been a great comfort to him. Most importantly, they are friends with whom he can be very honest. They come and tell him stories about Jesus, and he says to them words to the effect, 'I just don't know if he really is the Messiah. It's not quite how I was expecting it to be. I'm just not sure any more.' Those faithful friends go to find Jesus and tell him about John's deep questioning, and Jesus' response gives us an insight into his wonderfully understanding nature. Jesus might have responded by saying, 'Go and tell John that if he were a real prophet he would have no doubts about who I am. He has surely given in to the demon doubt, and there is no place for doubt in the heart of a man of God. Tell him to repent of his sin of doubt and ask God to have mercy on him.' However, there is no trace of judgment in Jesus' response to John.

Jesus knows John so well—they have almost certainly known each other since earliest childhood, since that moment when John leapt inside Elizabeth's womb when he sensed the presence of the unborn Jesus nearby (Luke 1:41). Jesus knows what John, that fiery prophet, needs to hear now. He needs to hear about signs and wonders, because John's currency is not subtlety—it is in the raw and powerful works of God, and in the clear preaching of the gospel. So the message Jesus lovingly sends back to John is all about the mighty and miraculous things that are taking place, and the free preaching of the gospel to the poor and downtrodden. That is all that John needs to hear. It will give him the strength he needs for his time of imprisonment and subsequent martyrdom. And what does Jesus say about this prophet who has his doubts? 'Among those born of women no one has arisen greater than John the Baptist' (Matthew 11:11).

Most of us have our days when our faith seems like it is on fire so that we feel we can achieve anything for the kingdom of God. And then, if we are honest, we have other days when faith feels much more fragile, and our life feels full of dark and disturbing questions. Most of life is lived somewhere in between those two extremes of burning faith and troubled doubt. While it is wonderful to enjoy those strong moments of bright faith, we need to be aware that seasons of doubt and uncertainty may actually be the times when deep faith is being forged within us. Our journey to deeper faith will almost certainly involve those moments when we say to Jesus words similar to: 'Are you the one?' and it is reassuring to know that when we do, Jesus is not shocked and disapproving. He will give us a personal message that will renew our faith. It may be conveyed as a verse from the Bible, a line in a book, a comment in an email, a scene from a film—indeed, in any number of ways. But it will be there, and it will be spoken in love.

Reflection

Think about moments of doubt in your life. What was it that helped you through? If you were to send a message to Jesus today, saying, 'Are you the one, or do I look for another?' what message do you think he would send back to you?

Prayer

Jesus, you show yourself to be a God who delights to find faith, yet understands our doubts. Kindle faith in my heart, not a superficial faith that is only concerned with knowing the right answers, but a faith that is forged on the cold anvil of doubt.

The In-between Times

When he [Jesus] had said this, as they [the disciples] were watching, he was lifted up, and a cloud took him out of their sight. While he was going and they were gazing up towards heaven, suddenly two men in white robes stood by them. They said, 'Men of Galilee, why do you stand looking up towards heaven? This Jesus, who has been taken up from you into heaven, will come in the same way as you saw him go into heaven.' Then they returned to Jerusalem from the mount called Olivet, which is near Jerusalem, a sabbath day's journey away. When they had entered the city, they went to the room upstairs where they were staying, Peter, and John, and James, and Andrew, Philip and Thomas, Bartholomew and Matthew, James son of Alphaeus, and Simon the Zealot, and Judas son of James. All these were constantly devoting themselves to prayer, together with certain women, including Mary the mother of Jesus, as well as his brothers.

ACTS 1:9–14

This, I think, must be one of the strangest episodes in the Bible. We are in the days after the resurrection. The disciples have lived through the most extraordinary few weeks. First, they endured the horror of the unfair trial and terrible crucifixion of Jesus. They had two nights of the deepest grief, and then experienced the wonderful joy of meeting the risen Jesus. This Jesus was exactly the same person as the 'old' one, and yet he was different, and the nature of his risen life was certainly very puzzling to the disciples. It became clear that he wasn't a ghost, even though he made his way through walls and locked doors; indeed, he was physical enough to be touched by Thomas, and he ate food with the disciples on more than one occasion. Usually, he was recognizable, but not always immediately, as Mary Magdalene and the two on the road to Emmaus discovered. Possibly the most disconcerting aspect of his resurrection self was that he would suddenly appear and then just as suddenly disappear. You might be having an evening meal in a locked room, and he was absent one minute and there the next; you would be walking along a road with him, call in somewhere for a meal and in the middle of the first course he'd be gone. I can't imagine the disciples ever getting used to this. In those days, they must have been always looking over their shoulders to see if he was somewhere nearby.

There was nothing unpleasant about these sudden appearances. From what we can see, every meeting was full of warmth and light and encouragement. The disciples would have remembered them most fondly. Then came the day of the ascension. Most of us reading this story know it so well, and we know what to expect, but did those first disciples? How much did Jesus explain to them about the ascension? Did he go into technicalities, explaining that he would literally rise up from the ground and just keep rising vertically until the clouds hid him? I don't think so. I get the impression that it totally mystified the puzzled yet faithful group of friends who witnessed this strange event.

Many have questioned the historical nature of the resurrection appearances and the ascension story, usually on the grounds that they are just too unlikely and go against all known laws of nature. Perhaps it's just my naivety, but I have never had any difficulty in believing these stories because I have always understood that the world after the resurrection would be a very different place. Before the resurrection, we had a world that was very predictable. After Jesus' resurrection, we entered a sphere of life that is beyond mortal understanding. Only the brain in a resurrected body would be able to grasp it, though the God-breathed instinct within us can sense something familiar about it. I suspect it all made little sense to the disciples. It probably felt as if the world they knew had lost its form and balance, and yet a deep instinct within them told them that there was a sacred place in the universe where all of this actually made sense, though they did not have direct access to it in their earthly lives.

Thus it was that for a short period of time, these disciples were growing into a new way of thinking with the help of the risen Jesus. Nevertheless, they were still surprised by the ascension. Jesus had spoken with them, given them final instructions and then he took off, literally. Of course, he could have left earth in any number of ways, and heaven isn't in outer space, but Jesus was trying to help his disciples accept the fact that he was now physically departing for the final time. They had to stop depending on a face-to-face relationship and prepare to relate to him in a new way through the gift of the Spirit that they were about to receive.

For a time, those disciples kept looking up at the sky. I wonder what was going through their minds. Before they had too much time to speculate, they were joined by two of heaven's messengers, who asked what seems a fairly silly question: 'Why are you looking up?' These messengers are there to help the disciples refocus and prepare for the coming of the Spirit of Jesus at Pentecost. They go back to Jerusalem, where they are joined by Mary and some others, and they pray and they wait. It must have been a time of great uncertainty. Would they have known exactly when the Spirit was going to come? Would they know *how* the Spirit would come? Would they know what would happen immediately after they had received the Spirit? My guess is that they did not know much about the details, but simply waited there in faith.

There is quite a lot of waiting and uncertainty in the Christian life. We can be faced with puzzling questions. We can be unsure what God is saying or doing in our lives, in our church or in our world. We can feel pretty vulnerable, especially if we are in leadership and people are looking to us to guide them. Yet such moments can be times of deepening trust, of drawing from stories of faith in our past as we prepare for God to do something new for our future. A new experience of Pentecost might come at any moment. It might even come today.

❖

Reflection

What issues in your life as a Christian puzzle you at the moment? You might like to spend a few moments holding this before God. Listen quietly as you do so. Listen to your rational thoughts, and also to those God-given instincts that are there to detect the messages and themes of heaven.

Prayer

Father, I have my moments when I am puzzled by what is happening in my life and by how you are leading me. Help me to know that such times of uncertainty can be moments of openness in which you may visit me through the gift of your Holy Spirit. Visit me, even today, as I wait on you.

Friday

Changed Convictions

About noon the next day, as they were on their journey and approaching the city, Peter went up on the roof to pray. He became hungry and wanted something to eat; and while it was being prepared, he fell into a trance. He saw the heaven opened and something like a large sheet coming down, being lowered to the ground by its four corners. In it were all kinds of four-footed creatures and reptiles and birds of the air. Then he heard a voice saying, 'Get up, Peter; kill and eat.' But Peter said, 'By no means, Lord; for I have never eaten anything that is profane or unclean.' The voice said to him again, a second time, 'What God has made clean, you must not call profane.' This happened three times, and the thing was suddenly taken up to heaven.

ACTS 10:9–16

Today's story is about Peter, and takes place after the experience of Pentecost. It is the Peter who is well recovered following the terrible experience of denying his Lord, and it is the Peter who has preached powerfully on the streets of Jerusalem, has been used by God for healings and miracles and is now a senior leader in the early Church. As we read this passage, it doesn't surprise us to hear that Peter has a strong commitment to personal prayer, and today's story describes a dramatic experience in one of his prayer times. He is staying at the home of Simon the Tanner, who lives in Joppa, which is known nowadays as Jaffa and is a suburb of Tel Aviv. Most likely, when Peter gets up on the roof, he is overlooking the Mediterranean Sea—it must have been a beautiful scene. Now, although Peter has become something of a spiritual superhero in the early Church, I find it rather comforting to discover that he is still very human.

Bear in mind that Peter is intending to pray, but we are told that he feels hungry, a situation not eased by the fact that lunch is being prepared downstairs and tempting aromas are rising to his prayer place. Yes, our superhero gets hungry like the rest of us. I've always imagined Peter to be a big man with a good appetite, and you get the impression in this story that his empty stomach was definitely distracting him from focusing on prayer.

Not only is Peter hungry, but he is tired as well, so he's battling both hunger and drowsiness, and in the end the warm air, beautiful scenery, smell of lunch and his weariness get the better of him, and suddenly he's asleep. Luke, the writer of the story, says he fell into a trance, and of course he did have a remarkable God-inspired visionary experience, but I can't help feeling that it all began with a moment of ordinary human weakness. In this vision, Peter is still on the roof of the house, and he sees a large sheet being lowered from heaven. As Peter looks into this sheet, he realizes that it has a most unusual cargo—it is a kind of Noah's Ark, filled with every kind of four-footed animals, birds and reptiles. Then a voice says, 'Get up, Peter; kill and eat.' Peter is no doubt thinking, 'Well, I know I'm hungry, but not quite *that* hungry.' Then he quickly becomes aware of a real problem here. The rules in Leviticus are quite clear: 'This is the law pertaining to land animal and bird and every living creature that moves through the waters and every creature that swarms upon the earth, to make a distinction between the unclean and the clean, and between the living creature that may be eaten and the living creature that may not be eaten' (Leviticus 11:46). Yet this voice is telling him that all should be killed and eaten. Peter has never touched unclean food, and how could God now be telling him to eat some?

Peter complains to the Lord, who returns with the words, 'What God has made clean, you must not call profane' (Acts 10:15). The vision repeats itself three times, just in case Peter is in any doubt. If you read on in the story, you will see that Peter ends up in a Gentile's home (forbidden for Jews), preaching the good news, seeing Cornelius and his family converted, and all receiving the gift of the Holy Spirit. Peter becomes convinced that the message of salvation is for all people, whether they are Jews or Gentiles, and this proved to be an immensely important message for him personally and also for the whole Church.

Most of us hold strong convictions that we have either inherited as part of our family or national culture, or that we have developed through our own personal experience and research. It can be immensely disturbing when our convictions are challenged, but we live in a world where passionate convictions can be the cause of terrible suffering. In the Christian Church, we have seen a long, sad history of Catholic and Protestant in conflict with each other. At the time of writing this book, I hear almost every day news of an atrocity somewhere in the Middle East, perpetrated by someone of strong convictions who cannot abide the presence of another person or people of different convictions.

Peter was not wrong to have his convictions. According to the ways in which God had led his people up to that time, they were absolutely right convictions. They were rooted in the law. But Peter had to have a visionary experience to show him that he must develop new convictions, ones that were rooted in grace. In Peter's case, it wasn't about abandoning his old convictions; rather, it was about listening to God at a deeper level. From time to time, it is important to hold our convictions before God, and ask him to speak to us about them. This involves quite a risk, because, as in Peter's case, his listening to God meant he had to re-evaluate completely a strong, lifelong conviction.

We can learn from Peter, who allowed the Lord to speak into his convictions and adjust them by his grace. This not only had benefit for Peter, but also opened a new gateway for the grace of God to be at work in the world.

❖

Reflection

Can you identify one of your strongest convictions? Try offering it to God in prayer and see if God wants to speak to you in some way about it.

Prayer

Lord, thank you for the convictions that are so important to me. I offer them afresh to you. Let me keep those that are truly of you, adjust those that need to be moulded by your grace, and be open to new ones as I discover more of your truth and love.

Honest Humanity

For we know that the law is spiritual; but I am of the flesh, sold into slavery under sin. I do not understand my own actions. For I do not do what I want, but I do the very thing I hate. Now if I do what I do not want, I agree that the law is good. But in fact it is no longer I that do it, but sin that dwells within me. For I know that nothing good dwells within me, that is, in my flesh. I can will what is right, but I cannot do it. For I do not do the good I want, but the evil I do not want is what I do. Now if I do what I do not want, it is no longer I that do it, but sin that dwells within me.

So I find it to be a law that when I want to do what is good, evil lies close at hand. For I delight in the law of God in my inmost self, but I see in my members another law at war with the law of my mind, making me captive to the law of sin that dwells in my members. Wretched man that I am! Who will rescue me from this body of death? Thanks be to God through Jesus Christ our Lord!

ROMANS 7:14–25

Frankly, this is not one of my favourite Bible passages! Paul's letter to the Christians in Rome is not only a masterpiece of theology, but it is also intensely personal, and we meet one of his really difficult personal struggles in today's reading. People reckon that the letter was written in the early spring of AD57 and it is probable that Paul was coming to the end of his third missionary journey, and was heading for Jerusalem. He is also anticipating visiting Rome, which of course he does eventually, though as a prisoner.

In the middle of the letter, he gets into the theme of God's design for us to lead holy lives, and in chapters 6 to 8 he writes a lot about the battle with sin. Over the centuries, Christian writers and preachers have written at great length on these passages. Some have used them as a basis for a theology that argues for every bit of our humanity being corrupt and wicked. Sadly, huge numbers of people have suffered as a result, and anything to do with humanness (especially sexuality) has been viewed with stern suspicion. I'm not convinced that this was what Paul was getting at here. Theologians will continue to discuss for a long time yet the nature of sin and human depravity. For now, I want to consider what was going on in Paul the human.

In this passage, it feels as if we have reached a vein of real vulnerability in Paul. He so loves Jesus and proclaims him as the Rescuer and Saviour of humankind, delivering us from sin and every form of corruption, and leading us into new life. From what we know of Paul, it doesn't sound as if he lived a particularly debauched life before he was a Christian. If anything, quite the opposite. He prided himself on living as a very upright Jew. We are not dealing here with someone who used to live a licentious life, got converted and looks with shame and horror on what he used to be like. No, Paul's problem is not to do with the past; it is to do with the present.

The fact is that he has been a Christian for some time now, and despite having had years of walking with Christ, knowing the love of his heavenly Father, and experiencing the glory of the Holy Spirit in his life, he *still* finds that there is a part of him that is interested in fairly unholy thoughts and activities. In these chapters from Romans, and especially as we get into chapter 8, Paul is working with the themes of flesh and spirit, which has given rise to the theology that is suspicious of anything to do with the body. Paul is very honestly recognizing that within his humanity there is a part that he calls 'flesh', and it profoundly puzzles him: 'I do the very thing I hate... For I do not do the good I want, but the evil I do not want is what I do' (vv. 15–19). He's not specific about what these things are, and we will never know. But we only have to ask ourselves what such things might be in our own lives, and we are probably fairly close to what it was for Paul.

Paul agonized over this. He so wanted to live a more holy life. He hated the inner conflict, and we sense his exasperation as he cries out, 'Wretched man that I am! Who will rescue me from this body of death?' (v. 24). Then, of course, he answers his own question: 'Thanks be to God through Jesus Christ our Lord!' Despite the fact that he is really struggling with part of his inner life, nonetheless he has found Jesus to be the one who is there as a rescuer.

Inner struggles of this kind can bring real uncertainty into our lives. We may go to church, pray, read our Bibles, but still we find pockets of resistance in our lives that seem resolved to oppose all our efforts to change them. Although Paul wasn't specific about his own struggles, I'm impressed that he didn't make out that he had no problems, and one of the lessons that I take away from this passage is the importance of sharing our struggles rather than pretending that we are a fully efficient glow-in-the-dark Christian. I'm never impressed by those who go to the other extreme and jokingly chat about their sins with others, as if God's not bothered. The fact is that he is a holy God, who gave his Son because of human sin.

What we need to acknowledge today is that Paul gives us an example to follow. He is honest about those things that get him down and defeat him. He is willing to tell others that he has his struggles, without glorying in it. If you read on into chapter 8, you will see that he also demonstrates wonderful confidence in the power of God to transform. The problem for us in today's culture is that if it doesn't happen instantaneously, we are not satisfied. God's work in us, on the other hand, is often very gentle and gradual.

Reflection

Read through this passage again. How much does it relate to your experience? Is there anything in your character or behaviour that exasperates you? You might like to read on into chapter 8 and be encouraged!

Prayer

Lord, you are a holy God, but I thank you that you understand my mortal nature, and that you love me as I am. Help me so to love you, that little by little I will become like your Son, Jesus.

Home (Blue)

Introduction

This week, we spend time thinking about the theme of home. A few years ago, I was on holiday with my family in Scotland, and we spent a day in Edinburgh. I decided to take them to have a look at the house where I was born. My family moved from this house 40 years previously, yet when I saw it childhood memories came flooding back. There was a man in the front garden, and when I started talking to him I discovered to my surprise that he was the man who had bought the house from my parents 40 years previously. He kindly showed us around the house. For me, it was a surprise encounter with the home in which I was born and spent the first seven years of my life. For my wife and family, it was just a house. There is a big difference between a home and a house.

Home is a theme close to all of us. We come from homes; we grew up in homes; our dreams are often located in previous homes; we live in homes. Our memories of home may be varied. Some may have painful memories, where home was a place of unkindness and abuse. Others of us are fortunate to have experiences of home that provide us with a store of good memories as we remember love, protection and safety. Others will also have known those good memories, but will have experienced the safety of home life shattered by tragedy or unwelcome events. Whatever our past or present experience of home, there is within us an instinctive sense that home is a place where we truly belong. We have lived in houses that have become more than buildings; they have become homes. But 'home' is more than houses: we talk about our 'home town', and our 'homeland'. Home is a place that is familiar; it is a place of safety, of welcome, of warmth. It is that place where we can truly be ourselves without risk or shame. It may be an idealistic notion, but it is one that is deep within us.

In our walk with God, the theme of home crops up from time to time. Times of change and renewal can cause us to reappraise where our real home is, and what the values of our home are. We can look again at what it means to have our 'home in heaven'. The colour blue may make us think of a clear blue sky on a summer's day, and something about looking at the sky can get us reflecting on our eternal home. Icon painters often liked to use blue to symbolize heaven. Renewal can bring a fresh understanding of our true home; conversely, as we think afresh about our true home—and realize that the kingdom of heaven is not just a 'house', but it is our 'home'—that in itself can awaken new life within us.

Memories of Paradise

Then God said, 'Let us make humankind in our image, according to our likeness; and let them have dominion over the fish of the sea, and over the birds of the air, and over the cattle, and over all the wild animals of the earth, and over every creeping thing that creeps upon the earth.'

So God created humankind in his image, in the image of God he created them; male and female he created them. God blessed them, and God said to them, 'Be fruitful and multiply, and fill the earth and subdue it; and have dominion over the fish of the sea and over the birds of the air and over every living thing that moves upon the earth.' God said, 'See, I have given you every plant yielding seed that is upon the face of all the earth, and every tree with seed in its fruit; you shall have them for food. And to every beast of the earth, and to every bird of the air, and to everything that creeps on the earth, everything that has the breath of life, I have given every green plant for food.' And it was so. God saw everything that he had made, and indeed, it was very good. And there was evening and there was morning, the sixth day.

Thus the heavens and the earth were finished, and all their multitude.

GENESIS 1:26—2:1

Today's reading takes us to the creation story. The opening chapters of Genesis are words that have moved both scientists and poets for many centuries. Somehow, the divinely inspired writers managed to capture the key messages in the creation story and at the same time record them so beautifully. No doubt the rather dry arguments about the origins of the universe will go on for years to come, and important as they are, we are not going to get into them today. We are going to reflect on the theme of home that we find here, in the first account of the creation of humans as recorded in the first chapter of the Bible.

God is busy making the universe, and towards the end of this process he decides to make humans 'in our image'. It's not the 'royal we'; this is the Trinity. Father, Son and Holy Spirit are going to create humans in their own image. Human community will be formed in the image of the holy Trinity. There will be Father–Son–Spirit features all over humankind. The first two chapters of Genesis treat us to a vision of the world before the dark influence of selfishness and evil have their devastating consequences.

So God does it. He creates humans, and in this version of the creation story we don't know how many. In chapter 2 it is the pair, Adam and Eve, so maybe it is the same here. And we are told that God blessed them. Humans are God-blessed in a way that nothing else in creation is. With the blessing comes a commissioning. God has created humans in such a way that the love between them will enable them to multiply. Here, in the very first moments of creation, there is a reference to sex! This infant community is also entrusted with the responsibility not only to reproduce human life, but to care for the earth and the creatures of the earth. That very thought alone is sobering as we consider the appalling way we have treated so much of God's creation. In the beginning, however, we did it well.

God also tells them that the whole earth is a well-stocked larder. It sounds as if life is vegetarian at first (we could go off at another tangent there!), and we can imagine a scene of perfect humans sauntering around a sun-warmed fertile land, enjoying each other and caring for the complex, beautiful and perfectly balanced world that the Holy Trinity has created. How hard it is for us to imagine that scene without it either becoming a cheesy Hollywood scene, or a setting for comic sketches and jokes. It somehow sounds rather fanciful, frankly almost beyond our imagining. And yet the writers were not playing around. However God constructed this astonishing creation, whatever processes it went through, whether it was a big bang or slow progression, the writers are making clear that at one special and almost unimaginable time, this world of ours and the people on it lived in perfection.

It always strikes me as strange that people are so keen to dismiss that idea. They neatly write it off as myth, as poets fabricating a story to make a point. But I can't quite buy that, and the reason is that I listen to an intuition that I find not only in myself, but also in others. I find a sense of 'there was once a better world', and it often goes with a longing, which is part hope, that 'there will one day be a better world'. And if God is involved, there is no reason why 'better' cannot mean 'perfect'. Laurens van der Post, author of *The Lost World of the Kalahari*, in which he showed how much he learned from indigenous peoples, was once interviewed by Richard Holloway. In the course of the interview, he revealed he nurtured a deep hope for heaven. When asked *why* he believed in heaven, he looked rather surprised at the question, and answered: 'Because of instinct, of course. We *know* it exists.' His experience of life led him to the belief that instincts did not need to be authenticated by academic knowledge in order to be respected.

There is no way that we can prove all of this, but we can spend time in the company of the creative blessed Trinity and listen to our own instincts, our own sense of our true home. On the seventh day of creation, God made the sabbath. This is the peak of creation, the day on which we let go of our duties and celebrate the good home that God has given us here on earth. It is also a moment when we can reflect on the paradise from which we have come and to which one day we will return.

Reflection

What is your feeling about the creation stories in Genesis 1 and 2? When did you last give time to reflecting, both with mind and feelings, on the way this world was fashioned and formed by God? If it was too long ago, spend a bit of time now and allow the Spirit of God to touch your God-blessed instinct.

Prayer

Lord, you created a world that is truly wonderful. As I look around it today, I grieve at how far from your ways we have strayed, and how much we have suffered by losing the vision of how it could be. Enable me to be a better steward, and may the vision of the home that is to come help me to make this home a better place.

Beyond Babylon

Listen to me, you that pursue righteousness, you that seek the Lord. Look to the rock from which you were hewn, and to the quarry from which you were dug. Look to Abraham your father and to Sarah who bore you; for he was but one when I called him, but I blessed him and made him many. For the Lord will comfort Zion; he will comfort all her waste places, and will make her wilderness like Eden, her desert like the garden of the Lord; joy and gladness will be found in her, thanksgiving and the voice of song.

Listen to me, my people, and give heed to me, my nation; for a teaching will go out from me, and my justice for a light to the peoples. I will bring near my deliverance swiftly, my salvation has gone out and my arms will rule the peoples; the coastlands wait for me, and for my arm they hope. Lift up your eyes to the heavens, and look at the earth beneath; for the heavens will vanish like smoke, the earth will wear out like a garment, and those who live on it will die like gnats; but my salvation will be for ever, and my deliverance will never be ended.

ISAIAH 51:1–6

Isaiah, like Jeremiah, was a prophet who first wrote to people threatened by exile, and then to those who were experiencing it. He lived in the eighth century BC, but the middle chapters of his book are highly relevant to the people in exile in the sixth century. Whether Isaiah foresaw this, or whether there was another prophet writing in the 'school of Isaiah', is a matter of some debate. For our purposes today, we shall simply note that our passage is of real relevance and importance to a people who are a long way from home.

Whether it is by direct insight from personal experience, or prophetic foresight, Isaiah sees clearly that the people of Israel are in a crisis in Babylon. Some have lost hope and their faith is weak. There are others who spend their whole time hankering after the good old days, and have no vision for the future. Then there are those who are starting to settle down in Babylon and, forgetting where they truly belong, try to make it home. Isaiah's task is to be a messenger of hope in a very difficult situation. He has to comfort those who are really hurting (hence the 'comfort my people' passage in chapter 40), but he also has to challenge those who can only look back, and whose lack of hope is causing them to settle in a land that is not their home.

In the passage we are looking at today, Isaiah very skilfully encourages those people to look back, but to do so in such a way as gives them vision for the future. It is as though he is calling them to step back and get a long-distance view. He takes them back to Abraham and to Sarah, the father and mother of their faith. Yes, by all means go back into your history, he says, but not so that you sit back and say, 'Those were the days.' Instead, look back to gain inspiration. The God who so greatly blessed them in the past has not changed. This same God will comfort Zion and renew her waste places, just as he visited Sarah who could not bear children and miraculously made her descendants as numerous as sand on the seashore. Isaiah then delivers God's promise that the wilderness will become like Eden. God is calling the people to remember their true home, that blessed land of fruitfulness. And then the Lord calls the people to lift up their eyes to the heavens and consider the earth beneath (v. 6). There is a call here to connect with our heavenly home and be reminded of its values of life, faith and hope; we are also to recall where we belong, where we are, and who we are truly meant to be.

Babylon can mean any place where we are oppressed, not free to be ourselves. It is a place of exile. If our Christian faith is a place of trudging and oppressive hard labour, then we are not home. And what happens then? Well, some in Babylon did attempt to settle down. They said, 'Well, it's not that bad. We can cope. Let's keep things as they are, because it looks like more hard work to make changes, and I'm not sure I want a long walk through the desert. It all seems impossible to me.' So we must listen to Isaiah, who tells us to look back at Sarah and Abraham. He uses the analogy of the quarry and urges us to go to this quarry and find the rock from which we were hewn. We will need to put on our hard hats, go up to those quarries and get a good reminder of the hills of faith that gave us life.

How do we know we are on a journey *to* home rather than *away* from home? Perhaps there are little signs: it's those moments when we feel we have come to our senses somehow; for a moment, we take our eyes off our ministry and look to the Lord, who calls us by name; when we find ourselves actually worshipping rather than participating in a nicely polished act of worship; when we push through the absurd fullness of the in-tray and discover a little of what it means when people say we are 'human beings' not 'human doings'; when we experience the Spirit of God touching us and despite our stuttering tongue and tired heart, we find ourselves preaching good news to the poor, and feel his anointing oil poured liberally over our weary souls, healing not only us, but others through us.

This is not about wishful thinking; it is about engaging in hopeful imagination. Our remembrance of our homeland fills us with hope, and helps us to find new ways of connecting with our story of faith in the past, but frees us to engage in the place we find ourselves now. We can actually sing the Lord's song in a strange land. In fact, we can sing it so well that it can transform the strange land we find ourselves in.

Reflection

Have a look back at the journey of faith in your own life. Is there a quarry that you need to revisit? Is there a message you heard then that you need to hear again today?

Prayer

Home-maker God, remind me afresh of where I truly belong. As a pilgrim in an often barren land, fill me with a sense of my true home, that the world where I live may become fertile with your renewing streams.

Tuesday

The Eternal Home

When the Lord restored the fortunes of Zion, we were like those
who dream. Then our mouth was filled with laughter, and our
tongue with shouts of joy; then it was said among the nations,
'The Lord has done great things for them.' The Lord has done
great things for us, and we rejoiced.

Restore our fortunes, O Lord, like the watercourses in the
Negeb. May those who sow in tears reap with shouts of joy. Those
who go out weeping, bearing the seed for sowing, shall come
home with shouts of joy, carrying their sheaves.

PSALM 126

This is a great homecoming psalm. The first half is a memory, and
the second half a prayer that comes out of the memory. It is a psalm
that does what Isaiah was calling for in our reading yesterday—
looking back and drawing strength from memories. No one is quite
sure what event the first few verses are describing. It could be about
people returning from the exile, or it could be deliverance from a
famine, plague, or attack by an enemy.

Whatever it was, the opening verses describe the immense sense
of relief experienced by a people who have been rescued. A community has suffered some kind of tragedy, but now their circumstances have dramatically changed, and they are experiencing the
kind of joy known in some dreams. They are utterly happy; they are
laughing and whooping for joy. Then surrounding neighbourhoods
become aware of this community's gladness. A comparison today
would be watching a nation celebrate after it has won the football
World Cup or European Championships. For the people of Zion,
there was no question as to who was responsible for this good

fortune: it was the Lord who had done great things for them, and the nations looking on also recognized the work of God.

If the first half of the psalm is a memory, the second half is a petition made during a tough time, which uses the memory as a kind of launchpad of faith. The writer of the psalm is clearly part of a community that has known a loss of good fortune. We don't know what it is, but whereas times were once good, they are now tough; we can imagine that there are people around with hangdog expressions, complaining about the pressures they are facing. So this psalm writer, through the prayer, gets the people to look back into their history, past their present difficulties. 'Remember how God delivered us once before. If he did it then, he can do it again.' With this in mind, faith rises and they can begin to pray with some confidence. And the prayer is a prayer of renewal—'Restore our fortunes, O Lord, like the watercourses in the Negeb' (v. 4).

The Negeb (or Negev) is a dry scrubland and desert area in the far south of Israel which merges with the Sinai Desert on the way to Egypt. Abraham and Isaac camped in various places in the Negeb, as did the Israelites before they settled in Canaan. The word 'Negeb' actually means 'dry' or 'parched', and it is renowned for its aridity and heat. It is a most inhospitable place for humans in the long, dry summer season. When the autumn rains come, however, the watercourses are filled again, and all kinds of plants and flowers flourish over a once-dead landscape. The prayer continues with another watery theme, as the writer thinks about sowing in tears. I find myself wondering quite what this means. Is it about a people sowing seed in a very hopeless situation, watching their few seeds going into a dry ground and not being sure whether they will survive? Or is it sharing a conviction that no tears are wasted, that in the sad process of grieving something is always sown that one day will bear a harvest? It is perhaps based in the wisdom that has looked at even the worst tragedies of life and seen that remarkable human ability not only to find healing of wounds, but to grow through difficult situations. However we understand this, the psalmist is sure that the end result is that one day we will come home. This is the destination of the psalm: home.

There are all kinds of experiences in life that make us feel a long way from home. If home is the place where we feel safe and loved, a place of belonging, then we are far from home whenever we feel insecure, uncared for, and where we have no sense of belonging. Sadly, too many Christians feel a long way from home, even in their own churches. Perhaps the joy and warmth they once knew doesn't seem to be there: for some, a cold formalism has crept in; for others, it has become a church that seems to cater for only one kind of people, and they don't fit into that category; for others, the church may not have changed, but they have, and this has changed their relationship with that church.

This psalm tells us that sometimes it is right to look back. Go back to that place in your Christian life when you felt so much at home. Think about it, not nostalgically because that only brings pain, but let your heart move from the memory of that happy experience to the God who gave that experience. He has not changed. Turn the memory into a prayer for renewal. It might run something like this: 'Lord, you did it then; now do it again. Something needs to change. Maybe it's them; maybe it's me; probably it's both. Come to the current dry places and bring autumn rain, and where I have been sowing in tears, lead me home with shouts of joy.' Such praying may not bring the immediate and full result we long for (though you never know with God!), but something happens deep in our hearts. We prepare the ground that has been hardened by despair or dull resignation, and seeds of hope are planted. And, to turn round an old saying, where there's hope, there's life.

Reflection

As you read about this theme today, what situation have you been aware of? What time of good fortune do you remember? Can you talk about it with God and describe the details of the experience? As you do that, turn the memory into a prayer of hope.

Prayer

Lord God, you have given humans the ability to remember as a way of holding in our hearts the life experiences that help to guide us in the present and shape our future. As we remember, so give us the grace also to hope, and to look forward with eagerness to those times of being truly at home.

When Jesus Is at Home

When he [Jesus] returned to Capernaum after some days, it was reported that he was at home. So many gathered around that there was no longer room for them, not even in front of the door; and he was speaking the word to them. Then some people came, bringing to him a paralysed man, carried by four of them. And when they could not bring him to Jesus because of the crowd, they removed the roof above him; and after having dug through it, they let down the mat on which the paralytic lay. When Jesus saw their faith, he said to the paralytic, 'Son, your sins are forgiven.'

MARK 2:1–5

The first chapter of Mark runs like an express train. The phrase 'and immediately' occurs several times, and episodes follow each other at a breathless pace. The last story of the chapter tells of Jesus healing a leper; news about this spreads so fast that he is swamped by people wherever he goes. Thus, we find him at the end of the chapter out in the country, or a 'lonely place' as some translations put it. Even there, however, people find him. You get the rather sad impression that there is nowhere now for Jesus to go where he can just have time to himself.

So he comes home. Jesus was born in Bethlehem, which was not his parents' home town; he spent some time as an infant in Egypt before moving to Nazareth, where he grew up. Nazareth was therefore his family town, but Mark tells us that Capernaum is the place where Jesus had his home. It's fairly unlikely that Jesus owned a property here, and the theory I like best is that Jesus probably made his home in Peter's house. Let's assume that this was Jesus' home base for his Galilee ministry. And we can assume that there must have been times when Peter's house, with his wife and possibly extended family around, was a peaceful resting place for Jesus (well, perhaps it was never that peaceful when Peter was around!).

In today's story, Jesus has slipped back from the country and is at this home in Capernaum, no doubt hoping for some peace and quiet. But it's not long before someone spots him. Did they see him through a window? Perhaps Peter's loud voice called out, 'Jesus, it's time for lunch,' and someone passing by heard, to the annoyance of those inside the house. Most likely, Peter's house, in common with others in Palestine at that time, would have its front door wide open during the morning, and passing friends would have dropped in and found that Jesus was staying there. One way or another, news gets round: Jesus is at home, and that means one thing to those who are troubled, sick, wounded, frightened, or inquisitive—Jesus is around to help. And it only means one thing to the paranoid, the controlling religious authorities, the ones who think they know how to communicate God to people—Jesus is around to cause trouble.

A mixed crowd, therefore, forms at Peter's house, comprising the needy, the inquisitive and the suspicious. In no time, a crowd has filled the house to capacity and jammed the entrance. Into this crowd comes a group of men carrying a paralysed man. As we saw earlier, when we were thinking about Peter and Joppa, the roofs of the houses are flat with an outside staircase, and this little group makes its way up to the roof. Peter can't be too thrilled to see his roof being seriously damaged, and possibly makes a few protests until he sees Jesus welcoming this group, who are making their unexpected and ingenious entrance. So it is that Jesus works his extraordinary and breathtaking miracle, and the man who was once unable to walk dances out, knowing he is healed and forgiven. If you read on in the story, you will see how the Pharisees, true to form, do not enjoy the miracle quite as much.

This is a story of Jesus at home. He is not a mighty preacher rolling up to a grand stadium in a black limousine surrounded by dark-suited minders. He's not the guest preacher in a religious building. He's just at home. It is so very normal, yet he's living the kind of life where you can just pop round and see him, and it was from his homely base that he taught and worked miracles of healing.

We can easily assume that home is too mundane a place for God to be at work. We imagine he needs somewhere far tidier, more religious and grander. And yet some of the most profound experiences of life happen in the home. I was born in my parents' home. Most of us, if we had the choice, would like to die at home. Brides often leave for their wedding from their parental home. Home is the place where the most serious and the most trivial exist side by side. And this is where Jesus loves to be. Sometimes we think we must search for renewal in places a long way from home. 'I must get out of this humdrum life and find a new world,' we might say. While it is true that adventures to new places can certainly bring experiences of renewal, today's story tells us that Jesus can work wonders in the ordinary world of the domestic home.

There's another point to ponder here, which is that our eternal home may not be so different from the good homes of this world. If I think of heaven, I find myself conjuring up rather silly images of huge palaces with marble staircases and long, echoing corridors. Maybe Peter's simple home in Capernaum might be much nearer the mark. Of course, we won't be too aware of the décor. We'll have our eyes on the one who has invited us to live there, and we'll feel more at home than we ever have done in our lives. That is a truly wonderful thought for those who have never known a safe or loving dwelling place in this life.

Reflection

Think about your present home. What do you think Jesus would do if you were to invite him to come in today? Where would he like to sit? What would you offer him to eat and drink? Let your imagination play with this thought and see where it leads you.

Prayer

Lord Jesus, please make yourself at home in my house. You know all who live here and all who visit. Help each one of us to encounter you, to listen to you and allow you to touch and heal our lives today.

Thursday

The Welcoming Father

Then Jesus said, 'There was a man who had two sons. The younger of them said to his father, "Father, give me the share of the property that will belong to me." So he divided his property between them. A few days later the younger son gathered all he had and travelled to a distant country, and there he squandered his property in dissolute living. When he had spent everything, a severe famine took place throughout that country, and he began to be in need. So he went and hired himself out to one of the citizens of that country, who sent him to his fields to feed the pigs. He would gladly have filled himself with the pods that the pigs were eating; and no one gave him anything. But when he came to himself he said, "How many of my father's hired hands have bread enough and to spare, but here I am dying of hunger! I will get up and go to my father, and I will say to him, 'Father, I have sinned against heaven and before you; I am no longer worthy to be called your son; treat me like one of your hired hands.'" So he set off and went to his father. But while he was still far off, his father saw him and was filled with compassion; he ran and put his arms around him and kissed him.'

LUKE 15:11–20

Today's story is likely to be very familiar to many of us. It is one of the best known of Jesus' parables, and only part of it is printed here. The second part of the story tells us more about the enthusiastic nature of the father's welcome of his son, and also the story of the elder son, who has very mixed feelings about the whole episode.

At the beginning of chapter 15, Luke gives us the context for a series of parables that Jesus tells, which are all about being lost and found: the Pharisees and the scribes are grumbling about Jesus' habit of mixing with 'tax collectors and sinners'. They are much put out that Jesus spends so much time with these irreligious people, and they feel it will bring their faith into disrepute. As Jesus tells these parables, his audience can be divided into two sorts of people: those who have lived a fairly irreligious life and know they have wandered a long way from God; and those who think they have done all the right things, yet in their hearts have travelled a long way from God, and don't realize it. So Jesus tells a story about two sons, and it is all about home.

The elder son loves being at home and is very dutiful. Like the Pharisees, he does all the right things. He knows the rules, how to behave and how to impress his father. As far as he is concerned, home is a safe place, where there are clear rules and if you keep these rules life ticks over very well. The younger son is full of spontaneous life; his experience of home is that he feels trapped and confined by the very rules that his brother likes so much. He hates the rules and formality, and he longs to break free. He has no money, though, and so he can't escape until one day he has the idea of asking his father for his inheritance. In so doing, he breaks a massive cultural rule. Any son who asked his father for his inheritance in this way was effectively saying that he wanted his father dead. It was one of the most disrespectful things a son could do, and most fathers would have been outraged and offended by such a request. This father is not like other fathers, however, and he gives his son his inheritance.

The son goes off and finds his freedom; however, it turns out not to be freedom after all, but a form of slavery. Eventually, he has no money left, and he ends up being treated like a pig, which in that culture is the lowest of the low. He realizes that life at home would be better than this. He believes that his father won't welcome him back as a son, but may have him back as a servant. At least he would have a roof over his head and food for his stomach. His experience of liberation from home has, paradoxically, taught him about the true freedom of home. When he returns, he encounters the unexpected unconditional love of his father, and home for him is a wonderful, safe place of welcome. Sadly, this act of grace has a terrible effect on the elder son: it exposes a large area of legalism and jealousy in his heart; it exposes the fact that although the elder son has lived at home, he has been a stranger—he has never really got to know his father.

As the tax collectors and sinners heard this story, they discovered there was a home to which they could return, where they would be sure of a celebratory welcome. There was a place where they belonged. As the Pharisees listened, they felt their safe home was being invaded. Areas of legalism and jealousy were being exposed in their hearts. Jesus' story has a place of welcome for them as well, though, for the father goes out to the elder brother and appeals for him to come in (Luke 15:28). His love for the elder brother is as strong as his love for the younger. He wants to bring them both home. Sinner and Pharisee are both welcome in the home of the Father in heaven.

The parable tells us that no matter where we might have journeyed in this world, there is always a welcome in our Father's home. For some, it may involve a journey from a place of sinfulness and carelessness; for others, it may involve a journey from a place where they've known the rules but not the Father. Wherever we come from, arriving home involves a fresh discovery of the love of God, and all fresh discoveries of the love of God open us to the streams of renewal.

Reflection

Imagine yourself in the story as the son or daughter of this father. Do you feel more like the elder child or the younger one? Maybe there is a bit of both in you. Do you feel close to home or far away? If you feel far away, imagine taking a few steps towards home today, and see if you can hear the words of the welcoming parent who is coming out to greet you.

Prayer

Lord, you are the parent who runs out to greet all your children. You are the parent who welcomes us home. You are the parent who is more interested that we are home than in accusing us for being away. You are the parent who dances with delight at our homecoming. Help me to believe this in my heart today, that I may journey home with confidence.

At Home in the Body

Not all flesh is alike, but there is one flesh for human beings, another for animals, another for birds, and another for fish. There are both heavenly bodies and earthly bodies, but the glory of the heavenly is one thing, and that of the earthly is another. There is one glory of the sun, and another glory of the moon, and another glory of the stars; indeed, star differs from star in glory. So it is with the resurrection of the dead. What is sown is perishable, what is raised is imperishable. It is sown in dishonour, it is raised in glory. It is sown in weakness, it is raised in power. It is sown a physical body, it is raised a spiritual body. If there is a physical body, there is also a spiritual body.

1 CORINTHIANS 15:39–44

1 Corinthians 15 is a fascinating chapter. It's all about resurrection, and focuses particularly on the resurrection of the body. Paul begins the chapter by reaffirming the mighty truth that Jesus was raised from the dead and appeared to many people. Clearly some people in Corinth, while finding they could believe in the resurrection of Jesus, were finding it much harder to believe that we humans would be raised from the dead too (v. 12). Paul gives much of the rest of this chapter to making very clear that humans are also destined for resurrection. In verse 20, Paul says that Jesus is the 'first fruits' of those who have died. In other words, he was the first to enter into this experience, and we who are in Christ shall follow one day.

In the Greek world, there was real anxiety about death. People believed in the immortality of the soul, but this belief was not connected to the body. Immortality was about getting rid of the body, not seeing it transformed. The news that this man Jesus had risen bodily from the dead was startling enough to the Greek world, but to add that humans would also have a resurrection body was even more mind-blowing. Not only was it very hard to believe, but it also seemed so unlikely. Could these mortal bodies, which cause us so much trouble in our lifetimes, actually be transformed after death in some mysterious way? This is why Paul has to give over a lot of his letter to explaining it to the Greek-influenced Corinthians.

The young Christians in Corinth are really inquisitive about this. They want to know *how* the dead will be raised (v. 35), and this question leads into the passage we are considering today. Paul gets quite expansive as he thinks about not just our mortal bodies, but animals, birds, fish, and beyond this world to the sun, moon and stars. The themes remind us of the creation story, where the immaterial God creates the most wonderful material universe. As Paul says, they are all glorious. There is no sense here that the spiritual is superior to the material. In the creation story, we see a beautiful interweaving of spirit and matter, body and breath, so Paul evokes that account as he tries to explain about the future condition of these bodies of ours.

The resurrection of the body is in the context of God renewing the entire universe, as he creates a new heaven and a new earth. We shall think more about this wider theme tomorrow; for the moment, we'll think about what is meant by this 'resurrection body'. Quite how it works is hard to imagine, but it seems clear from this passage that Paul is fully expecting some kind of remarkable transformation for our bodies after death. He invites us to consider what happened to Jesus. Just before he died, Jesus was weak, and the terrible damage done to his physical body eventually killed him. However, two days later he was around again in a spiritual body. As we have already considered, Jesus had a very physical body, yet at the same time it was most definitely a spiritual body, in that it came and went, appeared and vanished, and worked quite differently from the bodies of this world. Jesus was not a ghost because he had substance.

To put it another way, although the spirit has high value in this life, it is nonetheless somewhat limited by the body, which is restricted by the laws of nature (except where there is a miracle), and is subject to sickness and ageing. In the world to come, the spirit is no longer restricted by the body. Rather, the new resurrection body is subject to the spirit. It sounds wonderful!

Inevitably, in a largely scientific and somewhat cynical age, such notions seem quite foolish. Like the Greeks at Corinth, many people think such beliefs are eccentric, with no grounding in truth. I can't help feeling that there is something very important to grasp here, however. These bodies of ours will one day die and either be buried or cremated. But in Christ, there is an astonishing hope of some kind of resurrection, which is beyond the grasp of our mortal minds. This future hope affects how we feel about our bodies here in this world. Sadly, too many Christians are not at home in their bodies. We have already seen that, like Paul, we can get terribly frustrated by our normal human weaknesses. The fact is, though, that God has created these bodies of ours, and he expects us to take good care of them until the day they are transformed. What a wonderful hope that is, especially when we feel our aches and pains, and for those who struggle with debilitating illnesses.

In an earlier passage, Paul describes our bodies as temples of the Holy Spirit (1 Corinthians 3:16 and 6:19); they are holy and need to be treated with the greatest respect. A temple is well cared for when the God whom it serves is loved and respected. We may often feel the strains and stresses of this mortal life in our bodies, but it is worth remembering that they are temples of the Holy Spirit. They are places where God wants to be. They are bodies that will one day be gloriously transformed. Renewal is not just for the spirit—the Holy Spirit is quite at home in the human body.

Reflection

Spend a few moments thinking about what you have been taught in your life about the human body—were you taught to respect it, deny it, gratify it, hate it, love it? Whatever your experience, hold it alongside the truths in this chapter of 1 Corinthians and become at home in the body that God has provided for you.

Prayer

Lord, help me to treat well this body that you have given me for my life here on earth, so that it may be a worthy temple for the Holy Spirit, and thank you for that wonderful promise of a resurrection body.

The Home of God

Then I saw a new heaven and a new earth; for the first heaven and the first earth had passed away, and the sea was no more. And I saw the holy city, the new Jerusalem, coming down out of heaven from God, prepared as a bride adorned for her husband. And I heard a loud voice from the throne saying, `See, the home of God is among mortals. He will dwell with them; they will be his peoples, and God himself will be with them; he will wipe every tear from their eyes. Death will be no more; mourning and crying and pain will be no more, for the first things have passed away.'
REVELATION 21:1–4

There are times in our lives when these verses take on a special meaning, and very often this passage may be used at a funeral. For me, the passage came alive at the funeral of my Uncle Henry. He was a man loved by many people. He would freely acknowledge that a vein of pessimism ran through him, and yet you couldn't be with him for more than a few minutes before you were both laughing. In my case, our laughter often centred around some idiosyncrasy of the Church of England (we were never short of choice), mine from the vantage point of clergy, and his as a much-involved layman. Sadly, his life was brought to an end by a very painful cancer, and my father made regular visits to his bedside, where, even in his pain, my uncle would laugh with him as the two brothers recalled mischievous events of days gone by. These were not easy days for my father, as not only did he watch his beloved brother dying, but he was also caring for my mother, who was seriously ill with Alzheimer's disease.

Henry's funeral was held in an ancient little Buckinghamshire church on a hot summer's day, and we gathered for the funeral service full of grief and questions, as well as thanksgiving for such a good life. When it came to the Bible reading, my elderly father made his way to the front of the church, carrying the Bible he had had since boyhood, and he read to us from the book of Revelation. As he read, the weight of grief was almost too much for him, and he had to reach out to a nearby pillar for support as he read the words of this passage to us. It was an extraordinary picture—an old man, in an ancient church, reading from an ancient text that has been used for the last 2,000 years to remind us of our future home. His quivering voice proclaimed the good news—that one day, all this would change. There would be a new heaven and new earth; God would be living here, and the ocean of tears brought about by the death and pain of this world would be gone once and for all. I remember feeling those words like a cool breeze of hope, gently touching my aunt, cousins, family and friends. We knew instinctively, beyond the bounds of reason, that one day this transformation would happen, and it was this knowledge that made us a people of hope in the midst of our grief.

Sadly, for so many people the hope never gets much beyond being an undefined instinct. If we don't give it much thought, the instinct remains tantalizingly unclear, powerful though it may be. It simply joins the general amalgam of modern beliefs about life after death, including reincarnation and spiritualist ideas. The good news for the followers of Christ is that we have been given much more than a vague instinct. The writer of today's passage, John, was given the extraordinary vision that is recorded in the book of Revelation when he was in a place of lonely exile on the island of Patmos. There is much in the book that is hard to understand, but there is also much—such as today's passage—that is very clear indeed. No doubt John had given a lot of thought to the afterlife. He may well have been feeling his own frailty while in exile and considering his own death. But he was also thinking about this world—what was its future? How would it all end? Well, in his searchings he was given that extraordinary visionary insight, his Revelation.

He sees a new heaven and a new earth. How we would love him to have described these more, but no doubt their description could not be contained in words. As he sees this vision, he hears a voice that proclaims a message to the effect that God is coming home. If you think about this, it is truly remarkable. At the end of all things, we will not be travelling off to heaven, far beyond this solar system, this universe, this space; rather, God Almighty, the Creator of all things, is actually coming to live in a renewed earth. As he does so, he comes with healing—healing all the traumas, wounds, hurts, injustices, wars, crimes, sicknesses. He comes not as a remote, grand king returning from battle, but with immense tenderness and love, attending to each tear that has been shed on this earth.

If you start thinking about all this, it has powerful implications for so much in life. For example, it tells us that heaven won't be utterly and totally different from this world. If you move to a new house, you will be in a new building, but some aspects will still be the same—a building with walls, rooms, roof and so on. The new earth is going to be familiar, whatever its nature. It means that much of what we experience in this world will be in the next, except without the tears. And yet, of course, it will be wonderfully transformed, with God dwelling fully in the midst of it. Meditating on this theme will lead us to be filled with excitement at the thought of that new creation, with God so close and tears so far away. And it will also lead us to appreciate this world. I love Adrian Plass's poem 'Heaven' which begins: 'When I'm in heaven, tell me there'll be kites that fly.'[3] He explores the wonder of heaven by connecting it to the wonders of earth and ends with the words: 'I love this world you made—it's all I know.' God has given us a world to love and care for and a life to live well. But this is only the beginning!

❖

Reflection

How do you think this world will end? What are your thoughts about heaven? Read the passage again, and ask God to bless your imagination and see if you can get a glimpse of what this new heaven and new earth might be like.

Prayer

Come, Lord Jesus, come!

Creation (Green)

Introduction

We ended last week's readings thinking about the new earth that God will one day create, where he will make his home. This week, we take up the theme of creation, thinking in particular of this world that God has created, which will one day be transformed into the new heaven and earth. The theme of spiritual renewal has sometimes been seen as rather 'other worldly'. It has been supposed by some that the more renewed you want to become, the further away you need to get from this world. And yet, increasingly we are discovering that God's good creation is often the means of drawing us deeper into his rivers of renewal. There's a song I used to sing in my early days of being a Christian that began: 'Turn your eyes upon Jesus'; it encouraged us by saying that 'the things of earth will grow strangely dim' when we are in God's presence.[4] In recent years, I've come to question this a bit. As we shall discover this week, the Bible is very positive about many of the 'things of earth', which can be windows through which we can see Jesus.

When you see an icon that in some way depicts the Holy Spirit, you will often find the colour green. Take, for example, Rublev's famous icon of the Holy Trinity. The figure on the right is generally understood to depict the Holy Spirit, and he is wearing a green robe. If you go for a walk in the country in springtime, you are very aware of the many bright greens that are appearing. It is the colour of new life, or vigorous growth, and ushers in the return to the life of summer after the death of winter. Renewal is like springtime, a season when things come to life after a period of dormancy. It is important to remember, however, that spring is no better than other seasons. We need all the seasons, even winter. As T.S. Eliot wrote in his play *Murder in the Cathedral*, 'And the world must be cleaned in the winter, or we shall have only a sour spring, a parched summer, an empty harvest.'[5] There can be all kinds of 'winters' in our spiritual lives: times when it is hard to find life and inspiration from the Bible, prayer and worship. But sometimes, this can be a season where, stripped back to the basics, we discover new insights, and find strengths and abilities within us that we did not know we had. For many, an experience of winter is a natural prerequisite for a springtime of the soul. Few welcome such winters, but how worthwhile they are if they bring about a life-giving, renewing springtime!

A World Made by God

In the beginning when God created the heavens and the earth, the earth was a formless void and darkness covered the face of the deep, while a wind from God swept over the face of the waters. Then God said, 'Let there be light'; and there was light. And God saw that the light was good; and God separated the light from the darkness. God called the light Day, and the darkness he called Night. And there was evening and there was morning, the first day.
GENESIS 1:1–5

Those of us who live in busy, Western, commercial cities find ourselves all too easily removed from creation. I go to my supermarket and buy a frozen chicken, a tin of sweetcorn, a bag of chips, and, because I feel a bit guilty about the chips, I buy some bananas as a dessert, because I know I'm supposed to eat more fruit for a healthy diet. Then, a bit later as I tuck into a nice meal, I pause and think about the journey that has got all this to my plate.

Somewhere, an egg hatched and a young, fluffy chicken staggered around in its big, new world. If I've not bought a free-range chicken, then the chances are that this chicken grew up in a tightly packed shed until one day someone deemed it fat enough to attract my attention in a supermarket. Someone else killed it, plucked it and prepared it. From somewhere else in the world, a supply of packaging arrived and my chicken was smartly packed and put into a deep-freeze, until someone else took it to my supermarket.

Somewhere else in the world, probably a long way away, a farmer was growing corn, perhaps huge fields of it, sprayed against every conceivable disease and insect. Thus it grew and ripened under a hot sun, until someone came and harvested it. I don't know how they harvest corn. Did someone pick it for a very small wage, or did a sophisticated machine do it? And I have no idea how all those bits of corn come off the cob and end up in a nice lined tin on my supermarket shelf. As for the chips—well, they once started life in a field, but they don't look much like potatoes now, and I imagine that all kinds of things have been added to them in the process of their becoming chips. The banana is very nice, but I didn't check where it came from. All I know is that once, when I visited the island of Madeira, the tour guide described the once-flourishing banana industry, until someone in Brussels told them that their bananas were the wrong shape and the trade was devastated. My banana from my supermarket is apparently the right shape, so I'm allowed to buy and eat it.

A few years ago, I had a similar meal. This book is dedicated to Benjamin Muhalya, who lives in a remote village in rural Kenya. I stayed for a weekend at his home, and he treated me like royalty. He took one of his few chickens in the yard and killed it, plucked it and cooked it. He grew a little maize in his garden, and we ate that. We didn't have potatoes as he couldn't get hold of any, but we did have a few delicious (not Brussels-approved) bananas that were growing wild near his home.

What I noticed about Ben was that he lived in a state of harmony with creation. We ate our meal, sat outside his simple house and watched the setting sun and mist in the valley, feeling the God of creation ministering to us. Those who live near the earth know it better. They know its moods, its rhythms. They know its beauty and glory, and they also know its dark side. They know the cruel frosts, the brutal storms, the devastating floods and desperate droughts. Our creation is restless and in many places unhealed, waiting for the day when it will be totally whole. And yet, despite its wounds, it still manifestly displays the fact that it is formed and made by God, its Creator. Those opening verses of Genesis make it perfectly clear. Before God took action, there was nothing. It's impossible for us to imagine nothing, but there was a time when there was absolutely nothing. And then God decided that there should be something, so he created the heavens and the earth. The writers of those early chapters of Genesis leave us in no doubt that however God created the world, it was full of design and intention. Life began in a dark and formless way, but then through the wind of the Spirit and the word of God, the formless void was transformed into the best possible home for men and women, who were to be God's friends, and who would be entrusted with caring for the planet.

We know only too well what happened next. We look at our pollution-damaged world and feel full of guilt and sorrow. We see a multitude of dysfunctional humans, who, far from being friends of God, are striving and selfish, and make too many parts of our world a violent and tragic place to be. The opening stories of Genesis remind us of how life was meant to be. It is healing to get out into God's good yet broken world from time to time, to feel the earth beneath our feet and sense the force of the wind on our face. Try going outside on a clear night and lie on the grass, looking at the skies. Instead of imagining that they are above you, imagine they are *below* you, and that the good earth is holding you—feel its strength and security.

It is helpful to pause as we eat, and think about where our food has come from, reflecting on the kind of world that God has made, which supplies our needs. When we fill our car at the petrol station, it is good to think about the reserves of fuel that God has placed in our planet, reserves that we squander all too easily, yet reserves that he lovingly placed there. Such reflection connects us with our world, and can take us out of the busy, commercial humdrum of our lives and into moments of springtime renewal. Try it today!

Reflection

Think about what you expect to be doing in the next 24 hours. Are there opportunities where you can make a deeper contact with God's creation? Make a note to pause and reflect at those moments, and see where God takes you in your mind and heart when you do so.

Prayer

Dear Lord, as I consider this planet, set so perfectly in this universe, I am filled with wonder at your creation. Help me never to take it for granted, and make me a good steward of all that you have entrusted to me.

God's Voice in Creation

Ascribe to the Lord, O heavenly beings,
  ascribe to the Lord glory and strength.
Ascribe to the Lord the glory of his name;
  worship the Lord in holy splendour.
The voice of the Lord is over the waters;
  the God of glory thunders,
  the Lord, over mighty waters.
The voice of the Lord is powerful;
  the voice of the Lord is full of majesty.
The voice of the Lord breaks the cedars;
  the Lord breaks the cedars of Lebanon.
He makes Lebanon skip like a calf,
  and Sirion like a young wild ox.
The voice of the Lord flashes forth flames of fire.
The voice of the Lord shakes the wilderness;
  the Lord shakes the wilderness of Kadesh.
The voice of the Lord causes the oaks to whirl,
  and strips the forest bare;
  and in his temple all say, 'Glory!'

PSALM 29:1–9

I wonder what prompted the psalmist to write this wonderful song? No doubt the matter has been discussed and decided by scholars, but I can't help thinking that this psalm expresses one of those moments that are given every now and again when we are just gloriously gripped by the joyful wonder of God's power. Perhaps the writer had an experience of healing, or deliverance from some problem or other. Maybe it was someone who was out walking during a thunderstorm and became overawed by the majesty of God, displayed through the roar of thunder, the brilliant flash of lightning and the beat of heavy rain.

I remember once being caught in a sudden thunderstorm in the Valley of Rocks near Lee Abbey in North Devon. This valley acted like an amphitheatre for a spectacular heavenly play. For the first few moments of the storm, I desperately tried to recall whether I was supposed to stay away from trees or near them during a thunderstorm, and foolishly ran from tree to clearing while I made up my mind. In the event, I found a small building where I sheltered. I can't deny that I was quite frightened but also excited by the sheer power of nature, which suddenly made human efforts look feeble by comparison.

I think the psalmist may have had a similar experience, but whereas I was running for cover, I think this poet may have gone out into the storm and listened to the water and the thunder, and watched mighty trees struck by lightning. The psalm helps us to respond to the power of God in creation, for such manifestations of power can be understood as the voice of God.

The first verse encourages the heavenly beings to ascribe glory and strength to God, although they would need no encouragement to do so. Such power begins in the heavenly realms, but it doesn't stop there. The holy splendour of God visits earth, and actually works with the medium of the created world to communicate to us mortals. Rather than running for safety, we are invited to open our ears to hear the voice of the Lord in creation—and how powerful that voice is! It's so powerful that whole nations like Lebanon start skipping playfully in delight. God's voice is powerful in the lush forests of Lebanon, but it is also powerful in the barren wilderness of Kadesh. His voice is everywhere, and there's only one response: get into the temple and cry 'Glory!' When faced with the power and wonder of God, we are brought to our knees and give glory not to ourselves, not to creation, not to human powers, but to God Almighty.

It has long been part of Christian tradition to see creation as sacramental—that is to say, ordinary, earthly things can carry in them spiritual truths and messages. I heard a talk by Bishop Jonathan Bailey, recently retired as the Bishop of Derby, in which he spoke of 'holding creation up to the light to see the watermark of God'. It is a beautiful image that is full of meaning. Gerard Manley Hopkins writes:

> *The world is charged with the grandeur of God.*
> *It will flame out, like shining from shook foil.*

The poem includes a lament for the way we have treated the world, but then reminds us that despite our destructive ways, there still dwells in nature the 'dearest freshness deep down things', and it ends with a glorious affirmation of the work of the Spirit in creation:

> *Because the Holy Ghost over the bent*
> *World broods with warm breast and with ah! bright wings.*[6]

These lines encourage us to cast our minds back to that first story in Genesis, of the Holy Spirit brooding over the waters as a bird broods over her nest, nursing new life into being. This is the activity of the Spirit in and through creation.

As you read the Gospels, you become aware that Jesus often used images from creation to illustrate important spiritual truths. We shall look later this week at the imagery of seed and soil. I feel sure that the context for these kinds of parables might have been a journey that Jesus took with his disciples when he noticed a farmer sowing seed in a field. He would stop everyone and say, 'What's happening there?' and maybe Peter, a bit affronted by such a simple question, would reply rather sarcastically, 'A sower is putting seed in the ground. It's what you have to do.' Then Jesus would say, 'Now come on, Peter, look into this a bit more deeply. What's our Father in heaven saying through this? Look at those seeds on the path, for example. What's that saying to you?' And so it would go on, as Jesus taught his disciples to learn to listen to the voice of the Lord in his creation. He continues to teach us through his creation, if we will but listen.

Reflection

Think back over the last few days. Imagine that Jesus has been literally walking alongside you. At what point do you think he might have stopped you and said, 'Now have a look at that.' Once you have decided when that might have been, return there in your imagination, and ask Jesus to show you what he wanted to point out to you. Let the voice of the Lord speak to you.

Prayer

Lord, all too often my eyes are dim to your wonders, and my ears deaf to your voice, but let your Holy Spirit brood over my life with warm breast and bright wings, and let me hear your voice speaking to me through your good creation.

Creation and Worship

For as the heavens are higher than the earth, so are my ways higher than your ways and my thoughts than your thoughts. For as the rain and the snow come down from heaven, and do not return there until they have watered the earth, making it bring forth and sprout, giving seed to the sower and bread to the eater, so shall my word be that goes out from my mouth; it shall not return to me empty, but it shall accomplish that which I purpose, and succeed in the thing for which I sent it. For you shall go out in joy, and be led back in peace; the mountains and the hills before you shall burst into song, and all the trees of the field shall clap their hands. Instead of the thorn shall come up the cypress; instead of the brier shall come up the myrtle; and it shall be to the Lord for a memorial, for an everlasting sign that shall not be cut off.

ISAIAH 55:9–13

This chapter of Isaiah marks the end of that part of the book that is devoted to encouraging the people of God who find themselves in exile. It starts with the famous 'Comfort, O comfort my people' in chapter 40, and these final verses bring the passages of comfort to an end with a great song of praise and the message of hope of the journey home from exile.

We see in these verses that Isaiah is well accustomed to using the themes of earth to describe spiritual truths. He refers people to the height of the sky above the earth and says it's the same as the difference between God's thoughts and human thoughts. And yet that does not mean to say we'll never make contact with God's thoughts—quite the opposite. God's thoughts are conveyed through his word, and his word is like the moisture in the sky that forms as rain and snow on the high hills and makes its way down into the valleys, watering the ground, enabling seeds to root, grow and give food to humans, before the cycle continues with the moisture rising back up to the heavens again. It does not return empty, because on its journey it has done magnificent work in refreshing the earth and feeding God's people. In the same way, the word of God goes out from heaven and falls like dew on prophets like Isaiah, and waters the fruit of the prophecies that he gives to the people. In this natural cycle, the people hear the word and return praise to heaven.

As this beautiful passage continues, so the themes of creation are repeated, for as these hope-filled travellers set out again, this time not on a dreary trudge to exile, but on a celebratory return journey home, then the whole of creation joins in the praise. The mountains and hills will burst forth in praise, and the trees of the field shall clap their hands. It makes us think of the words of Jesus on his journey into Jerusalem. When the killjoy Pharisees want to forbid the crowd from celebrating, Jesus says that even if they manage to stop them, the rocks and stones would start shouting out for joy (Luke 19:40).

The early Celtic Church in this country loved the thought of God being active and alive in his creation. There is the well-known song of St Columba, which begins: 'Delightful it is to stand on the peak of a rock in the bosom of the isle, gazing on the face of the sea.' It is imagined that Columba wrote and used this as he stood on a beach on his beloved island of Iona, and the song uses the images of waves, beaches, tides, even seaweed in prayer and praise to God. This tradition remained part of the Christian faith, as it has existed in many parts of Ireland, Wales and Scotland. In the *Carmina Gadelica*, the collection of Celtic prayers and blessings assembled by Alexander Carmichael, there is a 'hatching blessing', said by a woman going to collect her eggs. The blessing opens with the following lines:

I will rise early on the morning on Monday
I will sing my rune and my rhyme.
I will go sunwise with my cob
To the nest of my hen with sure intent.
I will place my left hand to my breast
My right hand to my heart
I will seek the loving wisdom of Him
Abundant in grace, in broods and in flocks.[7]

This prayer is said by a person who has integrated her faith deeply with the rhythms of creation. She says the prayer as she makes her way to the hen-house to collect the eggs. The saying of the prayer means that it is not just an egg-collecting exercise. The normal everyday activity becomes an act of prayer and praise. As she travels to the nest, she holds her heart and her breast, as reminders of God's love and his provision. Just as she has loved and provided food for her children, so God is providing for her, through his love and through the hens. As she puts her hand in the straw looking for the egg, so she listens to God, seeking his wisdom. She is waiting to receive a word from the Lord to sustain her in her daily work and life. Such prayer is deeply renewing, because it takes the ordinary humdrum things of life and converts them into very special moments with God.

Reflection

Think of one of your normal everyday activities. Using the hatching blessing as an example, write a prayer that connects that activity with your life with God.

Prayer

Use the one you have written!

Streams in the Desert

The wilderness and the dry land shall be glad, the desert shall rejoice and blossom; like the crocus it shall blossom abundantly, and rejoice with joy and singing. The glory of Lebanon shall be given to it, the majesty of Carmel and Sharon. They shall see the glory of the Lord, the majesty of our God. Strengthen the weak hands, and make firm the feeble knees. Say to those who are of a fearful heart, 'Be strong, do not fear! Here is your God. He will come with vengeance, with terrible recompense. He will come and save you.'

Then the eyes of the blind shall be opened, and the ears of the deaf unstopped; then the lame shall leap like a deer, and the tongue of the speechless sing for joy. For waters shall break forth in the wilderness, and streams in the desert; the burning sand shall become a pool, and the thirsty ground springs of water; the haunt of jackals shall become a swamp, the grass shall become reeds and rushes.

ISAIAH 35:1–7

If you have a strong stomach, try reading chapter 34 before you get on to today's reading. It is a terrifying prophecy delivered to a people who have steadfastly set their faces against God; we hear that the Lord's anger has burst out over the nations of the earth. Isaiah delivers dreadful prophecies about the doomed being slaughtered and mountains covered in the blood of the slain. The chapter ends with a grim sense of desolation and you probably have little appetite for reading further. However, in chapter 35 there is a surprise: you hear the news that God is not just a God who hates sin, but he is also a God who is infinitely compassionate to his people. In these two chapters, you almost get the sense of God as an exasperated parent whose relentlessly misbehaving child has driven him to fury, but then he suddenly stops himself, sees a point of vulnerability in his child and runs to give comfort and encouragement.

The context for this wonderful passage of hope is a people who are in the most desperate of circumstances. It is written to those who frankly have only themselves to blame for the mess they are in, and it is likely that there are some who are very aware of that. When we find ourselves going through a tough time, it always seems doubly bad when we feel we are responsible. We are full of 'if only I'd…', and 'why didn't I…?' questions that poke and probe at us, adding regret and guilt to our already wounded souls. I guess that when Isaiah's first audience heard the terrible prophecies of his earlier chapters, some became very defensive and tried to justify their actions. But others would have responded with real humility. I think it is this group of very shattered, empty, contrite people, who would have been able to hear the prophecy in Isaiah 35 and taken immense heart from it.

The passage is rooted in the image of the wilderness, a theme that has always held significance in Christian spirituality. The Bible is full of great wilderness stories. Moses discovers the burning bush in the wilderness, and leads his people through the wilderness on that great 40-year journey to the promised land. There is also the story of Elijah in 1 Kings 19, going off to his wilderness place where he unexpectedly encounters God in a completely new way. In the New Testament, John the Baptist prepares the way of the Lord in the wilderness and our Lord Jesus goes off on his 40-day journey in the wilderness as a time of preparation for his ministry. Paul spent time in Arabia (Galatians 1:17) as he prepared for his ministry, and it is quite likely this included some time in the wilderness.

So much has been written on the significance of the wilderness, and so much could be said about it, but at its heart, the wilderness theme contains a simple message. The wilderness is the antithesis of a fertile, lush creation. Hold a picture of the endless sand dunes of the Sahara alongside a picture of an English riverside in May and you feel the contrast. We can become poetic about the wilderness, admiring its rugged beauty, but, to be honest, I think that if any of us had to live in it for a stretch of time, we would soon find ourselves hankering after water, greenery and signs of fertile freshness. Instinctively, we want to be where good support systems are in place, and where there are places of safety to which we can run should danger arise. It is the lack of those normal support systems and safe refuges that makes the wilderness such a threatening place.

In our Christian lives, we develop normal support systems. Reading the Bible, meaningful worship, lively faith-sharing and encouraging fellowship would probably be the kind of activities that Christians value as supports. But there are times when these are taken away. The Bible becomes a dull, difficult book; worship seems dry and fails to move us; we have no energy to share our faith, and other Christians seem distant. It is at these times that we may well feel that we are trudging out into the wilderness, and on particularly bad days we fear that our spiritual life is seriously under threat. There seems to be nowhere and no way to protect it. Will it finally collapse under a burning sun, starved of all that once gave it life? These experiences can be desperate and frightening. And yet, as the proximity of Isaiah 34 and 35 indicates, it can mean that we are only moments away from an experience of streams rushing into our desert.

In recent years, there have been a number of films produced under the general title of *Transformations*.[8] They describe a number of situations around the world where a desperate situation has been transformed by a visitation of God. Take Uganda, for example, a country that has suffered much at the hands of corrupt leadership regimes in recent years. Those terrible traumas drove good and faithful Christians to their knees, crying out to God to heal their country. The *Transformations* film on Uganda tells some wonderful stories of how people journeyed from a desert of terrible suffering to the sweet waters of renewal. The film in the series entitled 'Let the Sea Resound' tells the recent story of Fiji, a place that is viewed by Westerners as an ideal holiday location, yet a nation that has groaned under the weight of superstition and sorcery, tribal warfare and violent warriors regularly depopulating entire villages. The film tells the story of a Christian revival that is bringing the most unexpected and welcome healing to this wounded nation; it is expressed through an unprecedented unity among Christians who have come together in prayer and action that has resulted in rapid church growth and genuine socio-political transformation. The renewal has even affected the land and the sea, with very positive consequences for agriculture and fishing. No desert is a hopeless desert in God's plan. Any barren and apparently hopeless place can be transformed, for 'waters *shall* break forth in the wilderness' (my italics).

Reflection

As you think about your Christian journey today, is there a part of it that feels like a wilderness? If so, close your eyes and try to imagine how it looks. See yourself walking around in it, feeling the rocks underfoot and the sand running through your hands, sensing the dryness. Then speak those words, 'Waters shall break forth in the wilderness', and watch how the waters from God start to flow. Let God speak to you as you imagine this and listen to him.

Prayer

Lord, visit the deserts of my soul with your refreshing streams. Never let me lose my hope that rivers shall break forth even in the most arid wilderness, for in you any burning sand can become a pool, and any thirsty ground a spring of water.

The Seed that Dies

He [Jesus] also said, 'The kingdom of God is as if someone would scatter seed on the ground, and would sleep and rise night and day, and the seed would sprout and grow, he does not know how. The earth produces of itself, first the stalk, then the head, then the full grain in the head. But when the grain is ripe, at once he goes in with his sickle, because the harvest has come.'

He also said, 'With what can we compare the kingdom of God, or what parable will we use for it? It is like a mustard seed, which, when sown upon the ground, is the smallest of all the seeds on earth; yet when it is sown it grows up and becomes the greatest of all shrubs, and puts forth large branches, so that the birds of the air can make nests in its shade.'

MARK 4:26–32

There is something mysterious and wonderful about the transformation that a seed goes through when it meets the vital combination of soil, moisture and light. Perhaps you can recall as a child being given a little packet of seeds, and very carefully poking your seeds into the welcoming earth in a little pot. Perhaps within a few minutes you checked to see if anything had happened. After a few hours, it got a bit boring. Maybe, when no one was looking, you even poked that little finger into the earth again, just to check on how the seed was doing. After a day of disappointments, you were tempted to give up on the whole thing as a bad job. Then came that delightful moment: a tiny shoot of white and green started to push its way through the earth. Ever so slowly it straightened up and, yes, you could even make out a leaf forming. Thus, your first little seedling arrived. With that special capacity a child has, you probably had a moment of wonder and amazement. That funny little dead-looking seed had disappeared somewhere in the earth and in its place a young plant was growing. No matter how many scientists and biologists tell me why this is perfectly normal, there is still a child in me who is utterly amazed at this beautiful transformation.

This is the theme that Jesus uses in today's passage. It is a parable rooted in one of the great principles of creation: something dies and is transformed into something greater. Jesus tells of a person who sows seed in the ground. After sowing the seed, he leaves nature to her course, and goes about his everyday life, and in time he watches the seed sprout and grow, and like me 'he does not know how'. It is a happy mystery. Jesus explains that, all by itself, the earth does her work: she welcomes this little seed, cradles it and nurses it, until it dies in her arms, giving way to something new. She feeds that new little life; it grows first a stalk, drawn up by the warmth and light of the sun, until it instinctively knows that it has reached the point to produce fruit. Tiny seeds are formed in the head, and there it is: a full head of wheat. It's then, says Jesus, that the farmer goes out with his sickle, and cuts the ripe wheat that is his harvest. This, says Jesus, is like the kingdom of God.

I wonder if, at that point, some bold disciple said, 'Sorry, Lord, I don't quite get it', which led Jesus to add another parable to help. 'Well, think about a mustard seed,' he says, and everyone would know that the mustard seed was tiny, and they would also know that if you left it to grow wild it would become a very large shrub, so big that even the birds of the air could nest in it. I imagine the disciples' strained faces at this point. Yes, it's starting to make sense. I imagine them starting to grasp it: yes, there's something here about dying and rising, and something about things that seem so small and fragile being transformed into something very impressive.

In any kind of renewal, there is usually a measure of dying, and dying is something from which we instinctively recoil. Yet dying is at the heart of our faith. It was Dietrich Bonhoeffer who said, 'When Christ calls a person he bids them come and die.'[9] It sounds a bit bleak, but we have to keep remembering the seed. The seed could hang on to its present existence like grim death, so to speak. When it lets go, however, so much can happen, but it can only happen if it entrusts itself to the mothering earth, and trusts for heat and light to give it growth. This is what life in the kingdom of God is like: we commend ourselves into the parenting nurture of God, and trust him for the warmth and light of the Spirit to transform us.

Some time ago, a small group of friends and I were invited to move from one large, successful church to St Paul's, a much smaller, very vulnerable church, which had a tiny congregation of mostly elderly people. We sensed the call of God and we went. There were many deaths that we had to face: losing a church with which we were familiar; losing regular contact with good friends; losing a style of worship that was familiar; losing a sense of identity that we had from being part of our old church; losing a thriving children's and youth ministry for our families; some of us lost particular roles that we had in that church.

The people at St Paul's welcomed us very warmly, but they too had to die: they had to die to being a small, fairly tightly knit group; they had to lose a form and style of worship that they loved; they had to lose quietness in their services when noisy children arrived; they had to lose some of their traditions. Many deaths were taking place during that first year, and some still continue, and all of us have been faced with a question: do we risk dying and letting that new life come? How much easier it is to cling to what is familiar! And yet, vulnerable though we still are at St Paul's, we are seeing signs of new life. We are glimpsing the new shoots. Without warmth and light, those shoots will shrivel and die. All the time, we are dependent on the love of God, and love for one another, and we are dependent on the Holy Spirit, the water of life.

'Very truly,' says Jesus, 'I tell you, unless a grain of wheat falls into the earth and dies, it remains just a single grain; but if it dies, it bears much fruit. Those who love their life lose it, and those who hate their life in this world will keep it for eternal life' (John 12:24–25).

❖

Reflection

Think back over the past few months. Are there any areas of your life where you have had to 'die'? Can you see that 'dying' as being like a seed planted into the ground? Can you see signs of a new shoot growing from that seed?

Prayer

Lord, take whatever seed that needs to die now, and plant it in the good soil of your love. Then give me patience and hope in the waiting, and pour upon me showers of your Spirit, that I may see the plant grow, and much fruit yielded for the kingdom of God.

Groaning Creation

I consider that the sufferings of this present time are not worth comparing with the glory about to be revealed to us. For the creation waits with eager longing for the revealing of the children of God; for the creation was subjected to futility, not of its own will but by the will of the one who subjected it, in hope that the creation itself will be set free from its bondage to decay and will obtain the freedom of the glory of the children of God. We know that the whole creation has been groaning in labour pains until now; and not only the creation, but we ourselves, who have the first fruits of the Spirit, groan inwardly while we wait for adoption, the redemption of our bodies.

ROMANS 8:18–23

What an extraordinary chapter this is! Chapters 7 and 8 of Romans follow a rather similar pattern to Isaiah's chapters 34 and 35: one chapter has all the bad news, and the next all the good news. In the case of Romans, Paul has spent much of chapter 7 struggling with the problems of the law, sin and death. Then he bursts into chapter 8 with the opening verse, 'There is therefore now no condemnation for those who are in Christ Jesus.' It is the cry of a freed man, for Christ has dealt with sin; what's more, he has given the wonderful gift of the Holy Spirit to enable us to live a new life. A new life is no guarantee that we will be spared suffering, however, and in our passage today, Paul writes about the suffering in the world, and the relationship of the Holy Spirit to that suffering.

Almost inevitably, Paul has had to face the problem of suffering. If it has not been in his own life (for example the 'thorn… in the flesh' in 2 Corinthians 12:7), he has certainly seen godly faithful people suffer for one reason or another, and he has had to meet that old question, 'How can a God of love allow his people to suffer?' For example, he must have reflected on his experience of being present at the death of Stephen (Acts 8:1), and though he was not a Christian at the time, after his conversion he would certainly have thought about the cruel death of this faithful servant of Christ. In response to this problem of suffering, Paul firstly invites us to get a long-term perspective on this—a *very* long-term perspective. He points out that the sufferings we may experience in this world will seem very minor once we see the glory that awaits us in heaven. You can hear the cynics responding, 'That's all very well for you heavenly-minded holy man, but that blessed thought is not a lot of use to me while I'm racked with pain because of this illness.' I think that Paul has this kind of response in mind as he continues. He is thinking about the world we live in, this wounded creation in which there is so much struggle and difficulty. He is trying to get us away from a dualistic thinking of 'it's all terrible on earth and it's all wonderful in heaven'. In this passage, he is saying that there is a closer relationship between heaven and earth than that.

To help people understand, Paul personalizes creation. It becomes like an excited child, who is waiting for a favourite friend or relative to come round. They are standing on tiptoe to see out of the window, to catch sight of their visitor coming. In the same way, there's a sense of eager anticipation in creation, but what exactly is creation so eager to see? It can't wait for the 'revealing of the children of God'. What does this mean? Can you imagine this restless, wounded creation trying to catch a glimpse of a few people pleading: 'Make thy chosen people joyful' on a Sunday morning? Is that really what it's longing to see?

Well, Paul tells us that this creation is 'subjected to futility' and in 'bondage to decay'. The activity of death is strong within it. 'Futility' and 'decay' are strong words that are depressing when used in relation to 'creation', whose very nature is about life and vitality. The effects of evil and sin on this wonderful creation are truly horrendous. No wonder it is looking for rescue! The very humbling part of all this, which is almost beyond comprehension, is that it is humankind whom God is calling to be the rescuers. From the beginning, you and I were called to care for this amazing creation. It is a high calling indeed. The dreadful truth is that through our years of evolution and growing sophistication we have now reached the point that, with the press of a few buttons, we could destroy our planet. Also, even without pressing those buttons, but simply by continuing to release huge quantities of pollutants into our fragile atmosphere, we could make our planet terminally ill. Creation knows just how vulnerable it is to the selfish whims of its occupants. It knows that it needs help, and so it looks to the Spirit-filled believers, those who know they are children—the children who can cry out 'Abba, Father' (Romans 8:15). It is the humble children of God who can help, inspired by the Spirit who breathed life into this world.

I find it impossible to think of all of this without a deep sense of shame. There is no point in endlessly knocking ourselves for our failure to care properly for our planet, but it is important to be aware that as we enter into the life of the Spirit, sooner or later we are going to pick up the heart-cries of this beautiful but wounded creation. We, who are led by the Spirit, will want to bring healing to this planet entrusted to our care. Paul says we have the 'first fruits of the Spirit', that is, a foretaste of what is to come. A bit of heaven is given to us now to help us heal the earth, and this brings us back to the theme of the connecting of heaven and earth. To care for this earth properly, we need the help of heaven.

In Romans 7, Paul struggles with the effects of sin on his own life. In chapter 8, he widens it to the effects on the whole of creation. In our longing for renewal, we need to invite the Holy Spirit to come with healing and the message of forgiveness into our lives. As the Spirit visits us, so we are likely to sense the 'groaning of the Spirit' for creation. As we hear that groaning, so we hear the cry of creation, calling out to the Spirit-filled children for help. In response, we become very aware of our need of the resources of heaven supplied by the Spirit, as we are aware of our own frailty.

There is a cycle here about the Spirit, heaven, creation and our lives. When we are drawn into this cycle, it can lead us into unexpected avenues of renewal.

Reflection

If possible, find one of those pictures of our planet taken from space. As you consider the picture, dwell on the fact that this planet has been created by God as our home. What do you feel as you look at this blue-and-white globe? You may be surprised by quite strong emotions. What are these feelings saying to you?

Prayer

Father, your creation is standing on tiptoe to catch a glimpse of the children of God as they are revealed. When it catches sight of me today, may it not be disappointed!

Jesus and Creation

He [Jesus] is the image of the invisible God, the firstborn of all creation; for in him all things in heaven and on earth were created, things visible and invisible, whether thrones or dominions or rulers or powers—all things have been created through him and for him. He himself is before all things, and in him all things hold together. He is the head of the body, the church; he is the beginning, the firstborn from the dead, so that he might come to have first place in everything. For in him all the fullness of God was pleased to dwell, and through him God was pleased to reconcile to himself all things, whether on earth or in heaven, by making peace through the blood of his cross.

COLOSSIANS 1:15–20

Yesterday, we were thinking about the relationship of the Spirit with creation, and today we look at Paul's teaching on the relationship of Jesus with creation.

When I think about Jesus, I find I instinctively go back to the Gospel stories. I picture him strolling on a lakeside path with his friends, teaching them kindly about the kingdom of God; I see him bending down to take the hand of Jairus' daughter and miraculously bringing her back to life; I see him red-faced and fuming at the Pharisees; I see him horribly suspended on the cross, crying out to his Father; I see him surprising Cleopas and his friend on the road to Emmaus by his resurrection presence. In all of these images, he looks like a fairly normal man on the outside. In fact, many people of his day never got further than thinking of him as a man, so there was clearly nothing exceptional about his appearance, nothing indicating that he was God walking around on earth.

As far as we know, Paul never met the bodily presence of Jesus. He had his Damascus road experience, and in that experience met with Jesus. Paul believed he had had a resurrection encounter (1 Corinthians 15:8), and there is no doubt that he enjoys a deep and personal relationship with his Lord. It is in the context of that relationship that he explores the nature of this Jesus of Nazareth who taught in Judea and Galilee only a few years before Paul started his preaching tours. As the early Church gets under way, speculation grows as to just who this Jesus is. What does it mean that he is the 'Son of God'? In what way is he divine? For both Jew and Greek, this God–human was a mind-blowing phenomenon. Thankfully for us, Paul was unswayed by the latest speculations. He rooted himself in the scriptures and prayed deeply for the Holy Spirit to inspire his understanding, for Jesus had promised that this Spirit would lead people into all truth (John 16:13).

Inevitably, over time heresies arose regarding the person and nature of Jesus, and one such heresy was growing in Colossae. It is actually good news for us, because it meant that Paul in his letter provided some wonderful insights about Jesus and his relationship with creation. It is generally reckoned that some kind of Gnostic heresy was developing in the Colossian Church, and Paul needed to counter it with orthodox teaching. Part of this heresy was a kind of dualism that saw the physical creation as essentially evil, so Paul takes up the theme of creation at the start of this letter. Thus, he starts off: yes, Jesus is the image of God, who is invisible; God is not physical, but Jesus is the physical image of God. Right at the start, the physical dimension is affirmed. The whole fullness of God has always been—and always will be—in Jesus. Then he goes on to say that Jesus is the 'firstborn of all creation'. Jesus is there right at the very beginning, and it is in him that all things have been created.

'What?' you can hear the Colossians responding. All things created in that teacher from Galilee? 'Yes,' says Paul very firmly. And it doesn't stop there. All things have been created in Jesus (physical and spiritual), and they were also created through him and for him. Suddenly, this Galilean preacher is rather different from other contemporary preachers. In fact, he is different from all teachers past, present and future. Everything in creation has been forged through him and for him: the trees, the valleys and mountains, earwigs, turtles and mammoths, the moon, Saturn and Jupiter, galaxies beyond our solar system, as well as all the angels and spiritual powers in the universe, and all authorities on earth, governments, religious leaders—*all* created through him. We may have often intellectually consented to this extraordinary fact, but to take such a truth into our souls is a different matter. The implications are endless. And this is what Paul wants to convey.

Jesus' task in relation to this world is reconciliation, which he achieves through his death on the cross. This physical death has implications for the whole universe. In a way that I suspect will always be well beyond what our mortal minds can imagine, this Galilean carpenter's lad is the one who, through his death and resurrection, has started a process of healing and reconciliation. Paul tells us that this immense Jesus is also the 'head of the body', a term he uses to describe the Church. He is involving us in his work. His bodily presence is you and me, through whom he works by his Spirit to continue that task of reconciliation and healing for his broken world. In our longing for renewal, we need to spend time with this Lord of ours, become open to serve as part of his body, and engage in that reconciling task.

Reflection

Go back to today's passage, and imagine you are with Jesus somewhere in Galilee. Take the verses and speak them out as a prayer to him: You are the image of the invisible God, the firstborn of all creation; for in you all things in heaven... *and so on.*

Prayer

You are Lord. You are risen from the dead and you are Lord. Every knee shall bow and every tongue confess that you are Lord. Alleluia!

Surprise (Yellow)

Introduction

Most experiences of renewal contain an element of surprise. Life is going on relatively normally, and then something special and unexpected happens. Suddenly, the world feels and looks different. A letter comes through the post, or a phone call comes, and there is good news. C.S. Lewis chose to call his spiritual autobiography *Surprised by Joy*. In the book, he recorded his quest for spiritual joy and how, after spending much time rooted in atheism, he found himself journeying to theism and then on to personal commitment to Christ. He was utterly surprised by the direction of his spiritual journey.

Much of life is lived out in a world of normal routines, and its predictability can feel secure. There are times, however, when those routines can feel stifling, and we long for fresh air. Sometimes, they can carry with them heavy weights, and we long for deliverance. In C.S. Lewis' case, the routine included a sense of the absence of God and an assumption that he did not exist, only to discover that God patiently and lovingly pursued him and eventually made him aware of his divine presence. Lewis writes:

You must picture me alone in that room at Magdalen [College, Oxford], night after night, feeling, whenever my mind lifted even for a second from my work, the steady unrelenting approach of Him whom I so earnestly desired not to meet. That which I greatly feared had at last come upon me. In the Trinity term of 1929 I gave in, and admitted that God was God, and knelt and prayed: perhaps that night the most dejected and reluctant convert in all England.[10]

He was certainly surprised by his conversion, and his life took on a very different direction from that point, as he was to become one of the most articulate exponents of the Christian faith of the 20th century, whose works would be read by people all over the world.

In our readings this week, we shall be encountering several different experiences of surprise. God is the instigator of the surprises, revealing himself as a God who can make his presence felt unexpectedly in remarkable ways, and who can use the most unlikely of people in the most surprising ways. The colour for this theme is yellow. Yellow somehow seems right, because I see it as a splash of colour in an artist's picture that highlights a dramatic event. It is also the colour of the daffodil, that remarkable plant that appears just when winter seems to be going on for ever, and heralds the coming of a warmer and brighter world. The surprises of God are not always comfortable nor even welcome, but they are always heralds of warmth and light.

An Unlikely Hero

The Israelites again did what was evil in the sight of the Lord, and the Lord gave them into the hand of the Philistines for forty years.

There was a certain man of Zorah, of the tribe of the Danites, whose name was Manoah. His wife was barren, having borne no children. And the angel of the Lord appeared to the woman and said to her, 'Although you are barren, having borne no children, you shall conceive and bear a son. Now be careful not to drink wine or strong drink, or to eat anything unclean, for you shall conceive and bear a son. No razor is to come on his head, for the boy shall be a nazirite to God from birth. It is he who shall begin to deliver Israel from the hand of the Philistines.'

JUDGES 13:1–5

There is no doubt that Samson is one of the most surprising and unlikely leaders in the Bible. I think that if I had been writing the history of God's people, I would have skimmed over some of Samson's antics, and yet we actually know more about Samson than any other leader described in the book of Judges. Our passage today takes us to the beginning of the story of this wild man's life. We are told that it is a time when the Israelites are doing evil in the sight of the Lord. Those are bad days for God's people, as they are being oppressed by the Philistines. We are then told about a man called Manoah. As far as we know, he wasn't particularly distinguished in any way, but, like many before and after him, he carries a particular pain felt keenly by his wife and himself. They are without children.

We don't know the name of Manoah's wife, but there is no doubt that she is the hero in this part of the story. She may be greatly struggling in her sense of loss, but she must be open to God in some way because she is granted an extraordinary surprise—a vision of an angel. The angel of the Lord appears to her. We don't know how. Is she doing a household chore with her mind on the children she cannot have? Or is she striving in prayer, calling out to God to hear her? Or maybe she is asleep at night and suddenly woken. However it happens, the angel appears to her and announces that she is going to have a son, and also gives some details about the boy and how he is to be raised.

Mrs Manoah is part of that tradition of remarkable women who were mothers of great leaders, and who conceived them miraculously. Sarah bore Isaac; Rebekah bore Jacob; Hannah bore Samuel, and Elizabeth bore John the Baptist. Mrs Manoah believes the angel's news immediately, however unlikely it may sound. She knows that her God is a God of surprises and that with him nothing is impossible. So she goes to her husband to tell him the good news. He believes his wife, but if you read on in the story, you sense that he'd like just a bit more evidence. Thus, he asks the Lord for a return visit of the angel (v. 8), no doubt hoping that this time the angel will choose to visit him. Perhaps he's thinking of how his male friends might respond if he meets them for a drink after work one day and says, 'You'll never guess what! My wife's had a visit from an angel and there's going to be a miracle...'

Well, the Lord knows whom he can trust most in this situation, and he allows the angel to visit Mrs Manoah again, this time when she's out working in the field (v. 9). There's something of a humorous note in this story, as it's Mrs Manoah who sees the visitor, and then rushes off to drag her husband over to see the angel for himself. The angel duly hangs around and speaks with Manoah. While Mrs Manoah is quite happy to accept the authenticity of both messenger and message, Manoah himself is still struggling to believe this story and wants to know the angel's name. Why? Does he want to check it against a celestial register just to make sure he's not an impostor? The angel agrees to the offering of a young goat; Manoah burns the sacrifice, and the angel ascends in the flame. Even Manoah is in no doubt now that this is no clever human impersonating an angel, and finally (v. 21) he acknowledges that it is the angel of the Lord. Mrs Manoah had got to that point in verse 6!

So she gives birth to her son (v. 24), and calls him Samson which basically means 'sunny' (literally 'brightness'). In chapters 14—16, we get a series of stories that reveal the good, bad, ugly and completely wild aspects of Samson's personality. We may already know the stories well, of foxes with burning tails, riddles with lion carcases, deceitful Delilah, long hair and pulling down temples. It is action-hero stuff that all too often seems to come from a rather deranged man. And yet, surprisingly, very surprisingly, he is someone that God needs and uses in these times of Philistine oppression, and despite his curious ways, he is a man who burns with an inward longing for God and for his ways to be established on earth.

Mrs Manoah models for us one who is open to the surprises of God. In her case, the greatest surprise in her life comes at a time of personal sorrow and loss. Her pain does not cause her to settle into a state of ongoing despair, and there is a part of her that is open to hearing good news. She is able to receive the angel and believe him, in a way that Manoah cannot. Not only that, but she is able to raise and love her son, and live with the many surprises that his life brings to her. As I reflect on this story, I fear I am much more like Manoah than his wife. I like evidence. I like to be sure of where I stand. I like life to be reasonably predictable and safe. Surprises challenge all of this. Surprises may challenge our ability to believe; they may disturb our normal routines; they may challenge us to change; they may throw us more deeply on to God. There's no doubt that God does come to all of us from time to time, taking us by surprise and leading us into new patterns and pathways. At such moments, we can either respond with scepticism and questions, or we can surrender. Despite my preference for safety, I find increasingly that there's part of me that is saying more and more often to God, 'Go on—surprise me!'

❖

Reflection

Can you recall a time when you were really surprised by something? How did it feel? How did you respond? Was it a good surprise or a bad surprise? How open do you think you are to being surprised by God?

Prayer

Lord, even today, surprise me!

Love in a Foreign Land

She [Ruth] came and gleaned in the field behind the reapers. As it happened, she came to the part of the field belonging to Boaz, who was of the family of Elimelech. Just then Boaz came from Bethlehem. He said to the reapers, 'The Lord be with you.' They answered, 'The Lord bless you.' Then Boaz said to his servant who was in charge of the reapers, 'To whom does this young woman belong?' The servant who was in charge of the reapers answered, 'She is the Moabite who came back with Naomi from the country of Moab. She said, "Please let me glean and gather among the sheaves behind the reapers." So she came, and she has been on her feet from early this morning until now, without resting even for a moment.'

Then Boaz said to Ruth, 'Now listen, my daughter, do not go to glean in another field or leave this one, but keep close to my young women. Keep your eyes on the field that is being reaped, and follow behind them. I have ordered the young men not to bother you. If you get thirsty, go to the vessels and drink from what the young men have drawn.' Then she fell prostrate, with her face to the ground, and said to him, 'Why have I found favour in your sight, that you should take notice of me, when I am a foreigner?' But Boaz answered her, 'All that you have done for your mother-in-law since the death of your husband has been fully told me, and how you left your father and mother and your native land and came to a people that you did not know before.'

RUTH 2:3–11

The book of Ruth comes after the books of Joshua and Judges and just before the long history books of Samuel, Kings and Chronicles.

It is like a little romantic interlude, a story of real delight. We now know that Ruth is a very significant person, in that she is the great-grandmother of David and therefore an ancestor of Jesus (Matthew 1:1, 5), but at the time that the story happened, she was 'just Ruth'. The events of this story take place in the time of the judges which, as we saw in the story of Samson, was a turbulent time when the Israelites frequently did evil in the sight of the Lord and suffered as a consequence. There was often tension between the people of Israel and foreign neighbours, not least Moab (Judges 3:12–30). In fact there were times when there was much violence between the Israelites and Moabites, and the writing on a stone from that era (known as the Mesha Stele c.830BC) boasts of the massacre of entire Israelite towns. However, the story of Ruth comes at a time when there is peace between the two peoples.

The story begins when there is famine in Israel. A man from Bethlehem, called Elimelech, is so desperate for food that he de-cides to take his wife, Naomi, and two sons, Mahlon and Chilion, into the neighbouring land of Moab where they will be safe from the threat of starvation. Moab encompassed the great plateau east of the Dead Sea and contained large areas of pastureland that was excellent for grazing flocks of sheep and goats. We don't know how long the family lived there, but in time disaster struck, because Elimelech died and Naomi was left on her own with Mahlon and Chilion. Now well settled in Moab, the two sons met two Moabite women, Orpah and Ruth, and married them, and for ten years all was well again. Then, disaster struck again, as the two men died and the writer of Ruth sadly reports that 'the woman was left without her two sons or her husband' (v. 5). Naomi is now on her own without any blood relatives, but she has obviously grown close to her two daughters-in-law, Orpah and Ruth.

It is at this time that Naomi hears that the famine in Judah has come to an end, and so she sets out to return home. Instinctively, she includes Orpah and Ruth in this plan, as they have clearly become like daughters to her, and the sad group of three widows sets off for Judah. Then it suddenly dawns on Naomi what this means for Orpah and Ruth and she stops on her journey and says to them both, 'Go back each of you to your mother's house' (v. 8). Orpah decides to return. Then comes the first major surprise for Naomi. Despite her pleadings, Ruth is determined to stay with her. Naomi is all too aware of the serious implications of this decision, which will probably mean great loneliness for Ruth—a foreign young woman on her own in a land that has often been at war with Moab. It must have been a great comfort to Naomi to have Ruth staying with her, but when she arrives in Bethlehem at last, it is clear that she is still very depressed and feels that she has been the object of the Lord's affliction (vv. 20–21).

Thus, the two women settle in Bethlehem and, as we know, events then unfold into one of the great biblical love stories. Ruth meets Boaz who, happily, is not only a relative of Elimelech's, but a godly man with a kind and compassionate spirit. He is immensely impressed by Ruth's kindness to Naomi, and clearly very taken by her, and the love story progresses with the usual supply of anxious moments on the way to a happy ending. In the final chapter, we find Naomi no longer depressed and grieving but holding her grandson in her arms, something that at one time would have seemed totally impossible.

The story of Naomi and Ruth is full of surprises. Both of them found love in a foreign land—Naomi found the love of a daughter in Moab, and Ruth found the love of a husband in Judah. There are shocks as well—the famine, the exile and the sad deaths. Yet from this very unpromising situation, we see simple human love and the clear guidance of the God of love working in wonderfully transforming ways. Naomi was surprised and delighted by Ruth's love for her and her people—it was the beginning of a journey of healing for her. Perhaps Ruth surprised herself by the risk she was willing to take, but her love was stronger than her fear. Then she was surprised by the unexpected meeting with the kindly Boaz. Her potentially lonely life was transformed into one of love and fruitfulness. The God whom we love and serve does not keep us away from difficulties. We may often find ourselves in life situations that we would never have wished for—the loss of a loved one, an unexpected move to another town or community, the loss of the security of an income. Any of these changes can be very hard to bear. However, the book of Ruth reminds us that on these dark journeys we can still encounter the most unexpected and welcome surprises of God.

Reflection

Think about the way Ruth and Naomi both faced tragedy and disaster. What sustained them in the dark times? Think back over difficult situations in your life—what sustained you? Were there times when God surprised you with unexpected sources of help?

Prayer

Lord, when I find myself walking through days which feel dark and hostile, help me to remember that you are the same God who delighted Naomi and Ruth with unexpected sources of strength and help, and led them to warm and sunlit lands.

Visions by the River

In the thirtieth year, in the fourth month, on the fifth day of the month, as I was among the exiles by the river Chebar, the heavens were opened, and I saw visions of God. On the fifth day of the month (it was the fifth year of the exile of King Jehoiachin), the word of the Lord came to the priest Ezekiel son of Buzi, in the land of the Chaldeans by the river Chebar; and the hand of the Lord was on him there.

As I looked, a stormy wind came out of the north: a great cloud with brightness around it and fire flashing forth continually, and in the middle of the fire, something like gleaming amber. In the middle of it was something like four living creatures. This was their appearance: they were of human form. Each had four faces, and each of them had four wings...

Then the spirit lifted me up, and as the glory of the Lord rose from its place, I heard behind me the sound of loud rumbling; it was the sound of the wings of the living creatures brushing against one another, and the sound of the wheels beside them, that sounded like a loud rumbling. The spirit lifted me up and bore me away; I went in bitterness in the heat of my spirit, the hand of the Lord being strong upon me. I came to the exiles at Tel-abib, who lived by the river Chebar. And I sat there among them, stunned, for seven days.

EZEKIEL 1:1–6; 3:12–15

Today's reading is the beginning and end of the passage that describes Ezekiel's remarkable call to be a prophet. Ezekiel is a younger contemporary of Jeremiah and, like Jeremiah, he ministered to the Jewish people before and after the dreadful destruction of Jerusalem in

587BC. Ezekiel is a priest, and part of the sorry community that is exiled to Babylon; he therefore has a crucial role in helping the people to understand how God is at work in this totally unfamiliar land. In exile, he becomes a prophet, with the task of making sense of the disaster that has happened, and rebuilding the people's faith and hope for the future.

The first verse of his book refers to the 'thirtieth year', and it is likely that this is referring to Ezekiel's age. According to Numbers 4:3, a person entered the Levitical priesthood in his thirtieth year, and Ezekiel would have been very aware of this. The account begins with Ezekiel among the exiles by the River Chebar, which was a canal of the Euphrates near the city of Nippur, south of Babylon. It may have been a popular gathering place of prayer for the exiles. Was it by these rivers of Babylon that they sat down and wept as they remembered Zion (Psalm 137)? We don't know what was going through Ezekiel's mind at the time. All we do know is that while he was there, 'the heavens were opened' (v. 1) and he saw visions of God. I think we can be fairly certain that he had no suspicion that this was about to happen. He was probably very devout, and very prayerful, but it is most unlikely that he had ever encountered an experience quite like this. One moment, he was admiring the way the light played on the water, and the next the veil between this world and heaven was lifted and he saw things that few mortals had seen. It was a surprise of the most intense kind.

In the first verses of his book, Ezekiel attempts to describe these visions. He sees violent sandstorms and scorching flames, unimaginable creatures with fire passing between them, dazzling wheels that move in and out of each other and flow with the creatures, a throne of sapphire, a rainbow, the glory of the Lord; he hears the word of the Lord, commissioning him for his work among a rebellious people. Finally, he comes back to earth and finds himself with the exiles by the River Chebar, and he sits among them for seven days unable to say a word (3:15).

To say that Ezekiel was surprised by this vision would be one of the greatest of understatements. I am sure that he was very open to

God, but nothing could have prepared him for such a startling exposure to God's glory in all its fullness. Moreover, included in all of this was a clear call from God to speak to a people who had a strong track record of not wanting to hear what God had to say. No wonder Ezekiel was struck dumb for seven days. In some ways, he probably never recovered from the whole experience.

Ezekiel is not the only person to have had a visionary experience of this kind. True, his was particularly vivid, but there are many people who have known moments of openness when it seemed as if the veil between earth and heaven was temporarily lifted and they saw things in quite a new light. Sometimes a shock precipitates this. Many people find that vulnerable times in life, such as during the first shock of bereavement, give them an openness to 'seeing' in a way that they haven't before. Some people who have momentarily died on an operating table before being resuscitated have seen visions of heaven that have profoundly affected them. I visited the hermit and writer Brother Ramon in the last weeks of his life. About a month before he died, he was taken into hospital, collapsed while he was there and was then resuscitated. He told me that during those few moments between collapse and resuscitation he glimpsed heaven— he saw Jesus calling him over a bridge and he heard the words: 'All is love, all is life, all is light.' It was not his time—he had a few more weeks to go—but he told me that this experience gave him such certainty of heaven and the welcome he was to receive that it meant that he could die in a state of complete peace, which he later did.

We can't organize these kinds of surprises, but it is good to know that not far from us there is the world of heaven, a land of visions that are beyond our wildest dreams. Any of us at any time may be granted a glimpse. Maybe it will be to give us hope; maybe it will reveal a piece of God's plan for our lives; maybe it won't have any particular use at all, but is simply given because God is God and he is not confined to acting in ways that are only useful. Perhaps if we lived in the daily expectation that around any corner we might catch a glimpse of glory we would lead better and fuller lives, and be the better prepared for our final home.

❖

Reflection

As you think back over your life, can you identify any times when you felt that the veil was either lifted or at least a lot thinner than usual? How do you think you could be more open to God speaking to you in visionary ways?

Prayer

Vision-giving God, you who are all-glorious, thank you that you choose to visit us in our ordinary lives, sometimes granting us glimpses of heaven. Help me to be more open to your visits by day or by night, and when I see, help me, like Ezekiel, to respond with love and obedience.

Angels on the Hill

In that region there were shepherds living in the fields, keeping watch over their flock by night. Then an angel of the Lord stood before them, and the glory of the Lord shone around them, and they were terrified. But the angel said to them, 'Do not be afraid; for see—I am bringing you good news of great joy for all the people: to you is born this day in the city of David a Saviour, who is the Messiah, the Lord. This will be a sign for you: you will find a child wrapped in bands of cloth and lying in a manger.' And suddenly there was with the angel a multitude of the heavenly host, praising God and saying,

'Glory to God in the highest heaven, and on earth peace among those whom he favours!' When the angels had left them and gone into heaven, the shepherds said to one another, 'Let us go now to Bethlehem and see this thing that has taken place, which the Lord has made known to us.'

LUKE 2:8–14

Today's reading is about another revelation of heaven, but whereas the witness in yesterday's reading was a priest and one of the greatest prophets ever known, the witnesses in today's reading are far less distinguished. Around the time of the birth of Jesus, shepherds were despised by the religious authorities. They had to keep such a regular watch on their sheep that they were seldom able to perform the many duties required by the law of Moses, and were therefore regarded as unclean. To some extent, they were outcasts, and they must have been utterly astonished to be the recipients of this extraordinary heavenly visitation.

Luke tells us that the story takes place after dark. The shepherds were no doubt settling down for the night on a hillside outside the busy city of Bethlehem, and perhaps they were discussing the chaos in the streets during this time of the census. No doubt there was the usual banter about oppressive leaders, extortion by those making money out of the visitors, the weather, family troubles and so on. Perhaps it was one of those moments just before settling for sleep and they were looking up at the stars, when suddenly they were aware of a visitor—an angel of the Lord stood before them. There is no reason to suppose that they were experts on angels, or had experienced them before. It is very likely that they were shocked and terrified, and kept pinching themselves to see if this was reality or dream. Not only was there an angel standing before them, but also the glory of God was shining around them, a heavenly light that dispelled the darkness and rendered the light from the fire quite ineffective. Not surprisingly, they were terrified. It seems that angels are trained in the art of reassuring terrified humans, and this one managed to calm the shepherds. He said to them: 'I am bringing you good news—the Messiah has come, and he's here in the town.'

It really must have been the most extraordinary experience for these shepherds. In an age of much cynicism, it is hard for us to imagine what this was like. Those shepherds may have been unclean according to the strict religious rulers of the day, but it is very likely that they had their own dreams and longings for the Messiah as much as anyone. They would have talked about the day when the Messiah would come; they knew this would mean that at last there would be meaning in life and hope for the world. The Messiah would come to rescue, make good, put right. Yes, like many others of their time, they probably thought that that included ejecting the Romans from Judea and fulfilling other perfectly understandable human hopes. So when the angel told them that the Messiah had arrived, they would have been genuinely overjoyed and utterly amazed. Their dreams were coming true.

Then the angel said something rather curious: 'There's a sign so that you will know this is true: you will find the child, not in royal robes in a palace, but wrapped in cloths of poverty and lying in a cow's feeding trough.' Before the shepherds could respond to this, heaven exploded into a symphony of praise and the shepherds were now looking up not at distant pinpricks of stars, but at a company of angels who were singing at the tops of their voices—it must have been an overwhelming sound, and one which the shepherds no doubt kept in their memories for the rest of their lives.

Then everything went quiet and apparently back to normal. The shepherds were now in no doubt—the Messiah had come, and not only that, but God had chosen to send him into the world in a way that clearly communicated that he was for all people, not just the religious experts, the theologically equipped, or the materially powerful and wealthy. This was a Messiah for shepherds such as themselves—and for these men, this was unbelievably wonderful news.

There's a bit of me that struggles with this story. If I had witnessed such a remarkable heavenly fanfare, I think I would have wanted to see something rather more interesting than an everyday domestic scene of a mother nursing a baby and a father pushing bales of hay around and cleaning up after the donkey. I can't help feeling that the vision on the hillside was a lot more interesting than the scene in the stable. But the difference between those shepherds and me is that they had learned to 'see'. The hillside experience had opened their eyes to see an ordinary scene and understand a much greater meaning in that scene than what was immediately obvious. My sense is that as they told this story, probably many times over in the years to come, they were more excited talking about the baby than about the angels. Sometimes God surprises us with the spectacular in order to catch our attention. Once we are listening, there can be deeper truths to discover in the most ordinary and everyday scenes.

❖

Reflection

What would be the equivalent of that hillside for you—a place where you often find yourself? Imagine angels appearing to you in that place, filling it with their singing and their glory. Try to imagine what news they would want to tell you.

Prayer

Thank you, Lord, that you choose to catch our attention in so many surprising and wonderful ways. Make me open not only to the visions you may wish to give me, but also to seeing and hearing your messages in the normal, everyday scenes and events of life.

A Ghost on the Water

Immediately he [Jesus] made his disciples get into the boat and go on ahead to the other side, to Bethsaida, while he dismissed the crowd. After saying farewell to them, he went up on the mountain to pray. When evening came, the boat was out on the lake, and he was alone on the land. When he saw that they were straining at the oars against an adverse wind, he came towards them early in the morning, walking on the lake. He intended to pass them by. But when they saw him walking on the lake, they thought it was a ghost and cried out; for they all saw him and were terrified. But immediately he spoke to them and said, 'Take heart, it is I; do not be afraid.' Then he got into the boat with them and the wind ceased.

MARK 6:45–51

This story comes right after the miracle of the feeding of the five thousand. The disciples must have been in something of a state of shock as well as delight with that miracle. To see food miraculously appearing would be wonderful, but also immensely disturbing. There is a sense of safety in the laws of nature operating normally, but when the unexpected happens, upsetting our expectations, we can feel very insecure. So the disciples are still reeling from one miracle when they encounter the next. When all the leftovers have been gathered up and sorted, Jesus tells the disciples to get into the boat and go over the lake to Bethsaida, where they have more work to do. No doubt, he tells them that he needs to be on his own for some peace and quiet to pray to his Father, and they will not begrudge him his need for space. Jesus goes up the mountain, and the disciples launch out on to the water.

Let's think of the story firstly from Jesus' point of view. Mark tells us that he is up on the mountain, praying. In John's account of this story, he tells us that some of the people wanted to make him king after the feeding of the five thousand (John 6:15). Perhaps Jesus needed space to return again to his Father, to resist any temptations for worldly glory, to pray for people to have a proper understanding of the Messiah, and not to use him to satisfy their own need for power. You get the impression that he worked hard in intercession during the night, but this time of intercession was broken when he became aware of his disciples. Mark tells us that he 'sees' the disciples. Does he actually spot them from his hillside vantage point, or is Mark referring to seeing with the perception granted by the Holy Spirit? Whatever it is, he is suddenly concerned for them, and he goes off to see them, which involves walking on top of the water. There's a part of me that wonders whether, tired by the exertions of the previous day's work and a night at prayer, he overlooks the fact that his walking on the water might cause some alarm to the disciples. It doesn't seem to occur to him that they might be rather taken aback by this sight! Mark then tells us that he intended to walk on by. You really do wonder what was going through Jesus' mind at this point. What's the point of going out to help them, if he's only going to walk by them—and where is he going to? Perhaps it simply shows that he would only come to their boat if invited.

From the disciples' point of view, the story starts off as a routine trip across the lake. Not all of them are fishermen, but for those who are, this is familiar territory. Not long before, they have been earning a living from these waters. The lake is their ordinary, everyday world. No doubt, as they row out with the sun setting, they are chatting about the day's events. At some point, the wind starts to get up and the water becomes rough. There's no sense in this account that the disciples are in danger, but they are clearly finding it very hard work. So here they are, back in their old world, and it feels a hard slog.

Then something weird and frightening happens. Just as the light is starting to break, they see a figure on the water. Mark tells us that they are in the middle of the lake, so there's no chance that it is someone wading in the shallows by the shore. It is a human who is actually walking on the surface of the water. In recent days, the disciples have been growing used to unnatural happenings, but this must be one of the most bizarre things they have yet seen. Their only explanation, understandably, is that it is a ghost. It may be in their minds that ghosts appear to those who are just about to become ghosts themselves, in their case by drowning in the storm. It is no surprise, therefore, that they are terrified. At that moment, they hear a familiar, reassuring voice, and it dawns on them that this is not the figure of a ghost, but the living person of Jesus, who is speaking to them, telling them not to be afraid. He comes towards them, climbs into the boat, and as he sits down among them, the wind ceases. I imagine for a few moments there is complete silence, both on the lake and in the boat, and as the sun rises, the disciples slowly start rowing again and make their way to the shore.

This is a story that is both disturbing and comforting. It is disturbing to know that we love and serve a God who is frankly very unpredictable, who does not seem to conform to the rules and laws that we would like to construct for him. He is a God who can be apparently absent at a time of need, and then frightens us by his sudden and surprising appearance. At the heart of this story, though, is the praying Jesus, in tune with his Father, looking over our world and seeing when things are getting rough for us. At those moments, he comes walking out to us, unperturbed by the wind that has made our life such hard work. He walks near our rocking boat and whether we ask politely or scream in terror, he understands our invitation to come to our aid. It is when he settles beside us that we notice that the wind is abating and life has become easier. We would never wish for the rough and stormy times in our lives, but it is so often true that in those moments we receive surprising visitations of Jesus that can make all the difference.

❖

Reflection

As you think back to times when life has become a hard slog, can you think of how Jesus came to visit you? Was it through a friend, a Bible verse, a sense of his presence? If life seems hard work for you today, think back over this story and use your imagination to see Jesus coming to you across the troubled waters, bringing his presence and peace.

Prayer

There are times, Lord, when it feels as if I am rowing into a strong head wind and I feel weary. Come and surprise me during those times, so that I may know your presence with me.

A Hurricane in the House

When the day of Pentecost had come, they were all together in one place. And suddenly from heaven there came a sound like the rush of a violent wind, and it filled the entire house where they were sitting. Divided tongues, as of fire, appeared among them, and a tongue rested on each of them. All of them were filled with the Holy Spirit and began to speak in other languages, as the Spirit gave them ability.

ACTS 2:1–4

Luke begins his Acts of the Apostles with one of the resurrection stories of Jesus (Acts 1:4ff.). It is about an occasion when he was eating with the disciples. I love the way the risen Jesus still involves himself with everyday activities such as eating. I get the sense that by now the disciples are getting used to Jesus popping up unexpectedly, and maybe they always had a spare dinner available, just in case. Anyway, on this occasion Jesus tells them that they must stay in Jerusalem and wait for the Father's gift, that he will baptize them in the Holy Spirit. Soon after that, Jesus is 'taken up to heaven' (v. 2). The disciples must have been used to surprises by now, but even they would have been mystified by this vertical disappearing act. They are profoundly puzzled, but thankfully there are two angels at hand to give them some guidance (v. 10).

The disciples are aware that Jesus has gone, and will come again in glory one day soon. Until then, they must wait in Jerusalem for the fulfilment of his promise. How much do they understand about this promise? I think that the evidence we have about the disciples tells us that they often don't grasp the meaning of what Jesus is saying. When Jesus tells them in verse 5 that they are to be baptized in the Spirit, do they understand what that means? The next time they speak to Jesus, they ask whether this is the time when Jesus will return the kingdom to Israel (v. 6). That sounds as if they believe that the promise of the Father and this 'baptism of the Spirit' is something to do with Jesus coming with battalions from heaven to rescue God's Rome-oppressed people and bring the longed-for freedom. Is this what they are expecting when they go to wait in Jerusalem?

In that time of waiting, they get on with the practical matter of choosing a replacement for Judas, and Matthias is elected. Luke tells us that they are also praying—in fact, they are 'constantly' praying (v. 14). The apostles are there, as are a number of women, including Mary, the mother of Jesus. How I would love to have heard her praying! This is the last time we hear of Mary in the Bible, and I have always liked that record of Mary: 'Last seen in a prayer meeting.' I think that is very fitting for her. From what the Gospels tell us about her we know her to be a deeply spiritual and prayerful woman, with an instinctive understanding and acceptance of the things of God. She had proved herself as an obedient servant. She had been through the terrible experience of seeing her son cruelly and publicly murdered. She had marvelled at his resurrection, and had long accepted that though she was his mother she could have no special claims on his life. She was utterly giving and was now open to God doing whatever he would, in and through her. She must have been a wonderful influence in that prayer meeting, and I imagine that when some zealous enthusiast got it a bit wrong and prayed for Jesus to come in mighty power to slay the Romans and return the kingdom to Israel, she would knowingly and lovingly look to heaven and simply pray for the coming of the Spirit.

So there they all were—a group of men and women who had known Jesus, listened to his teaching and who were doing all they could to be faithful to him. They were in Jerusalem at another great festival—Pentecost. The last great festival, Passover, had been utterly dreadful for them as they witnessed the death of their Lord. They were still in mortal danger because if, at the last festival, the religious leaders managed to kill Jesus, there was every possibility that they would now target his followers, especially with the rumours of resurrection flying around the city.

It is this group of puzzled, frightened yet hopeful men and women who are about to be surprised by the Spirit. They are praying on the festival day, when suddenly a roaring sound fills the room. They describe it later as sounding like a mighty wind. It roars around the house where they are meeting, and yet nothing is blown over. It is a wind, but not a physical kind, a mere current of air. And then, even more curious, great bursts of flame appear in the room and then separate out and hover above each person gathered there. It is perhaps an intense and personal expression of that manifestation of glory witnessed in the temple when Solomon blessed it (2 Chronicles 7:1–3). Whatever it is, as the disciples receive it they know that they are being filled with the Spirit of God. They can feel it—there can be no doubt about it and they do what all humans do when they are filled with joy: they shout, speak and sing. Only it is not their usual language that comes from their lips; it is a heavenly language, a language of the Spirit, uncontrolled by laws of literacy, unconfined by the limitations of vocabulary. It is a language of freedom, where love can be expressed without restrictions. Then, filled with the Spirit, they burst through the doors out into a waiting world and start the work that has been going on for 2,000 years since, the work of proclaiming Jesus as Lord.

There are many debates about Pentecostal experience, but this story has an essentially simple message: God sends his Spirit to prayerful, humble people who long to make his love known to a lost and hurting world. The first distribution of the Spirit to the Church was certainly dramatic, and there have been many similar expressions down the ages. For others, the Spirit is given in different, quieter ways. It is God's Spirit, and he chooses to give as he wishes; the chances are that we will often be surprised, and we will also be surprised at how God uses us as he baptizes us (which literally means 'immerses' us) in the life of his loving, holy Spirit.

❖

Reflection

Think about whatever experiences of the Spirit you have had. How have you changed as a result? How much do you long for more of the Spirit? What would you like the Spirit to change in your life? You may like to use the words of the prayer below as a prayer for personal renewal in the Spirit.

Prayer

Come down, O love divine,
seek thou this soul of mine,
and visit it with thine own ardour glowing.
O Comforter, draw near,
within my heart appear,
and kindle it, thy holy flame bestowing.

BIANCO DA SIENA, d. 1434, TRANSLATED BY R.F. LITTLEDALE (1833–90)

Surprised by Basics

For this is the message you have heard from the beginning, that we should love one another. We must not be like Cain who was from the evil one and murdered his brother. And why did he murder him? Because his own deeds were evil and his brother's righteous. Do not be astonished, brothers and sisters, that the world hates you. We know that we have passed from death to life because we love one another. Whoever does not love abides in death. All who hate a brother or sister are murderers, and you know that murderers do not have eternal life abiding in them. We know love by this, that he laid down his life for us—and we ought to lay down our lives for one another.

1 JOHN 3:11–16

The last reading for this week takes us to one of the letters of John. The author of this letter does not tell us who he is, but the early Christian leaders understood it to be written by John, the son of Zebedee (Mark 1:19–20). Jesus had nicknamed the two brothers the 'Sons of Thunder', which suggests a fiery temperament. This fiery nature is seen in the story where they want to call down fire from heaven on the Samaritans (Luke 9:54). It was these two who went to Jesus to ask if they might sit at his left and right in the future kingdom (Mark 10:35–41). Not surprisingly, the rest of the disciples were somewhat indignant about the brothers' bid for glory, and Jesus takes the opportunity to teach them all about humility. John is one of Jesus' closest disciples, and he grants him access to moments of great intimacy. Only Peter, John and his brother James were taken by Jesus to the Mount of Transfiguration (Matthew 17:1). The brothers are again found with Jesus in the

Garden of Gethsemane, but they are unable to face the pain of this moment and retreat into sleep. John witnesses the horrors of the crucifixion and later runs to the tomb to discover that Jesus is raised from death.

In John, you have on the one hand a man of great passion and zeal for holiness, and on the other a man who has been close to some very vulnerable moments in Jesus' life, and he has seen some of the depths of the love and compassion of God. Predominant in John's heart and mind is the message of love, and his letter rings out a clear message that Christians should love one another. He tells his readers that this is the message they have heard from the very beginning. It is nothing new; it is not a fashion; it is not an option; it is there at the heart of our faith. John emphasizes this by talking about the direct opposite, using the first story of hatred in the Bible, where Cain murdered his brother Abel (Genesis 4.8). These two were brothers—they knew that the very nature of brotherhood was to love and care for each other, and yet evil invaded Cain's heart and he murdered his brother Abel because of jealousy.

In this passage, John tells his readers that they should not be surprised if they find the world behaves like Cain towards them. They are likely to be recipients of hatred, because evil stalks the world and is threatened by the Christian community where the love of God is active and blazing out like light into darkness. I wonder whether the first readers of this letter began to feel a little uncomfortable at this point. John was a very senior and respected leader, and they would agree with him, and yet perhaps they were aware that he was exposing one thing that they were refusing to face: the fact that they did not love each other. Had they got to a point where frankly it was hard work loving some people in the way Jesus had commanded, and perhaps some were saying: 'Well, it's just human, isn't it?'

John crashes into this complacency by saying, 'Whoever does not love abides in death.' The more I think about it, the more I am not only surprised, but shocked and disturbed. Can this really be true? What about all that un-love I see in the Church, all that coldness, suspicion, backbiting and so on? I went to a church recently that had known grievous division. One person told me sadly about a fellow worshipper who deeply resented him. He longed for reconciliation, and during the communion service went over to shake hands during the sharing of the peace, but when he touched the other person he was told to get his hands off him, or else: 'I'll have you for assault.' What would John have said? He would have described that person as a murderer. It's as stark as that for John, because love is so important.

This may come as a surprise to some, but the fact is that loving one another is not an option taken up by rather holier-than-thou people who are naturally forgiving, while the rest live in the 'real world'. John makes it clear that love is at the very heart of our faith, and it is essential to our witness. John had heard the words of our Lord: 'By this everyone will know that you are my disciples, if you have love for one another' (John 13:35). We live in a world where terrible suffering is caused by people who do not love one another. Whether it is domestic violence, parental abuse, bullying by peers, or (on an international scale) terrorist atrocities and the terrible consequences of our failure to love our developing-world neighbours, we see a world desperately sick because people live in the death of lovelessness. In response, God sent Jesus to show us the way of love, and Jesus sent his Spirit so that normal humans could be empowered to live differently. It is desperately sad that the community that God has commissioned to be bearers of his love takes so lightly its failure to fulfil this calling. Some renewals begin with our being shocked into seeing the coldness of our hearts, so that we respond by crying out to God to visit us with his love divine.

Reflection

Go back over today's passage again and read it slowly and thoughtfully. How do you feel as you read it? What situations in your life does it make you think of? What would John say to your church if he were writing to it today?

Prayer

Lord, all too often I fail to love as you have commanded, and I am truly sorry. Send your Holy Spirit to my heart today, for you can visit even the coldest places of our lives and transform them.

Passion (Orange)

Introduction

In many churches, the Sunday two weeks before Easter is known as Passion Sunday. It is that point in Lent when we start to focus more specifically on the suffering of our Lord and prepare for our annual remembrance of the events leading up to his crucifixion and resurrection. Mel Gibson chose to call his film about the last hours of Jesus' mortal life *The Passion of the Christ*, no doubt because the primary theme was the personal suffering of Jesus. The word 'passion' comes from the Greek word *pascho* (meaning 'I suffer'), from which the word 'paschal' derives, as in 'paschal lamb' (see, for example, 1 Corinthians 5:7). In Christian tradition, therefore, the word 'passion' is linked with the suffering of Jesus. In our modern world, however, the word has developed in meaning. If you mention 'passion' to most people today, they will assume you are referring to sexual love. In some ways, the concept now seems a long way from personal suffering, but presumably the word developed in meaning because it was recognized that deep feelings, even deep feelings of love, have an element of pain in them.

Christianity has often been presented as a very passionless religion, particularly when it is displayed in formal churches. Go to an Anglican evensong or a choral matins, and you will find that emotion is seldom displayed, even though it might be deeply felt. Charismatic and Pentecostal churches can be judged to be over-emotional by those who like their Christianity decent and in order. As we shall see this week, however, deep feelings are very present in the Bible and are often displayed. Also, passion is a vital part of renewal. Renewal should be holistic, which means it will affect us in body, mind and spirit, and each of those involves our emotions.

Orange is our colour this week. It is a bright and distinctive colour, full of life and energy, and speaks of the emotional vitality that the Spirit brings to our lives. We shall be looking at a range of feelings and drives within us, and how they relate to renewal. It is not an exhaustive range, but it is enough to show that any renewal will have an emotional content, and that renewal often begins with our being stirred emotionally.

Longing for Renewal

The hand of the Lord came upon me, and he brought me out by the spirit of the Lord and set me down in the middle of a valley; it was full of bones. He led me all round them; there were very many lying in the valley, and they were very dry. He said to me, 'Mortal, can these bones live?' I answered, 'O Lord God, you know.' Then he said to me, 'Prophesy to these bones, and say to them: O dry bones, hear the word of the Lord. Thus says the Lord God to these bones: I will cause breath to enter you, and you shall live. I will lay sinews on you, and will cause flesh to come upon you, and cover you with skin, and put breath in you, and you shall live; and you shall know that I am the Lord.'

EZEKIEL 37:1–6

We return to Ezekiel, that prophet in exile who was open to the most wonderful and extraordinary visions. In today's story, he is transported to a valley by a combination of the hand of the Lord and his Spirit. It is clearly a visionary experience, and yet it is described so clearly that it feels as if Ezekiel is literally there. He arrives in this valley and we get a vivid sense of its dry and desolate nature, not least because it is full of bones. What a dreadful scene it must have been, because we know from later in the story that these are human bones. It would be like arriving on the scene of some brutal massacre or terrible plague that happened many years ago. There is a sense of tired history, of tragic loss and of grim hopelessness. The Lord leads Ezekiel around the valley, and we can imagine him wandering slowly through it, every now and then kneeling in the dust and touching a bone and discovering how terribly dry it is. There is no sign of life anywhere. As we read the story, we can almost smell and taste the stale, dry air.

Then God asks a perfectly absurd question: 'Mortal, can these bones live?' If he had asked me, I would have answered, 'No, Lord. No way—bones only live in cartoons and fantasy films. This is the real world, where bones just do not suddenly spring to life.' A bit of me would be relieved to have been asked a fairly easy question by God, but then I would also know that questions from God seldom have straightforward answers. Ezekiel is wised up to this—he's been a prophet long enough to know that you don't give an obvious answer to one of God's questions, so rather diplomatically and skilfully he replies, 'Well, Lord, only you know the answer to that.' I wonder what Ezekiel thought would happen next. Maybe he expected to be told to do the respectful thing and bury those bones and let the dead rest in peace. But God then gives him a command that must have startled him. He is told to prophesy to these bones —to speak to them; to speak in such a way that they will hear and respond. The idea is utterly ludicrous. I mean, for a start, their ears had rotted away long ago, so they have no mechanism to hear the prophecy. And we can't even entertain the insane possibility that the dead can come back to life. This is not Ezekiel's response, however. He does exactly what God asks of him. And why does he do this? Because it accords so much with the desire of his heart. As he has been wandering around these bones, he has been longing to see them come back to life.

God is able to entrust this vision to Ezekiel because, as a true prophet, Ezekiel is longing for the righteousness of God to be revealed. He has been working prophetically among a very broken people. He has seen the dreadful collapse of the city of Jerusalem, and the death of just about every hope that the people of God once cherished. He has sat with them by the waters of Babylon and watched them weep. Everywhere he goes, life feels like an extended funeral, and something within Ezekiel is telling him that this cannot be the end of the story. When he finds himself in this valley, therefore, he knows what to do. He calls out, no doubt with a booming voice that echoes in the hills surrounding the valley, 'Dry bones, hear the word of the Lord…' for the word of the Lord will bring life wherever it goes. If you read on in the story, you will read how those bones responded, and how Ezekiel prophesies to the four winds, which turn a heap of bones into a vast army. The Lord tells Ezekiel that the bones are the people of God who have been saying, 'Our bones are dried up, and our hope is lost; we are cut off completely' (v. 11). God promises to breathe his Spirit on his people, 'I will put my spirit within you, and you shall live' (v. 14). As you read this, you cannot but feel lifted by a wonderful sense of hope.

There is something about a desperate situation that connects us to a place of deep longing in our souls. I was ordained on a bright September morning in 1978. I walked out of Christ Church Cathedral in Oxford, on to the sunlit lawns, and I felt confident that I was going to serve in a church that was being renewed by the power of the Spirit, and that I would see in my ministry a mush-rooming of dynamic, loving churches across the land. It was at a time when charismatic renewal was waking up many individuals and churches, and there were many reasons to be hopeful. In the years since my ordination, though, I have witnessed a terrible haemorrhaging of life from the Church of England, particularly of children and young people. The statistics do not make comfortable reading. Thankfully, there are pockets of life that are very en-couraging, but the overall situation is still far from good. There are times when I feel that, like Ezekiel, I also walk through a valley of many bones. It is at times like this that I locate within my soul a raw and desperate yearning. It simply wants to cry out again and again for the four winds to come and raise up a mighty army that is able to battle against the forces of darkness that cause such pain and conflict in our world. I think we all have our longings, but too often they become submerged under the heap of the normal everyday pressures of life. From time to time, however, the hand of the Lord lifts us up, re-engages us with our longings, and moves us into a dynamic realm of prayer and prophecy.

❖

Reflection

What longings do you hold in your heart? Does the image of the valley of dry bones fit with this longing? Or is there another image that fits better?

Prayer

Holy Spirit, visit the place where I keep my longings, and help me to listen well to you so that I may know how to pray for the fulfilling of the deepest desires of my heart.

Power of Intimacy

O that you were like a brother to me, who nursed at my mother's breast! If I met you outside, I would kiss you, and no one would despise me. I would lead you and bring you into the house of my mother, and into the chamber of the one who bore me. I would give you spiced wine to drink, the juice of my pomegranates. O that his left hand were under my head, and that his right hand embraced me! I adjure you, O daughters of Jerusalem, do not stir up or awaken love until it is ready! Who is that coming up from the wilderness, leaning upon her beloved? Under the apple tree I awakened you. There your mother was in labour with you; there she who bore you was in labour.

Set me as a seal upon your heart, as a seal upon your arm; for love is strong as death, passion fierce as the grave. Its flashes are flashes of fire, a raging flame. Many waters cannot quench love, neither can floods drown it. If one offered for love all the wealth of one's house, it would be utterly scorned.

SONG OF SOLOMON 8:1–7

It has been a matter of considerable embarrassment to the Church down the ages that a book like the Song of Solomon (sometimes called 'Song of Songs') actually exists in the Bible. Even if you try and allegorize it, you're still faced with the fact that it is a love song in which the lovers write fairly explicitly, albeit poetically, about their desire for each other. I have heard lengthy expositions on how this is a love song of Christ for his Church; I have no doubt that the book can be understood in that way, and that part of its purpose is to help us discover more about Christ's love for his bride. Most are agreed, though, that the book was first written as a simple and beautiful love song between two people, who were utterly besotted with each other and who could hardly wait for the consummation of their love on their wedding night.

It always strikes me as strange how the Church developed a reputation for being anti-sex. The Jewish faith has always offered a very well integrated way of life, holding together body, mind and spirit. When the Church in the first few centuries of its life chose to distance itself from its Jewish roots, a dualism started to creep in, unhelpfully separating body from spirit, and things to do with the body were regarded with great suspicion. From this emerged the conviction that it was improper to give too much attention to sexual matters. Indeed, some early Christian leaders actually developed a theology arguing that Eve's act of rebellion was to have sex with Adam. Thus, sex was seen as something full of danger. Holy people remained celibate, but some had to marry to prevent them from falling into sin, and also to help populate the world. This view is typified by the Book of Common Prayer 'Solemnization of Matrimony'. At the start of the service, the priest warns that marriage is *not* 'to satisfy men's carnal lusts and appetites, like brute beasts that have no understanding', and goes on to say that marriage was ordained first 'for the procreation of children', second 'for a remedy against sin, and to avoid fornication', and third 'for the mutual society, help and comfort, that the one ought to have of the other'. Such a public statement at the beginning of the wedding service is not exactly a positive commendation of sex! It is disappointing to think that the Church could easily have retained the healthy attitude to sex that is present in our Jewish heritage. Instead, we are left with a Church which has always given the impression of being rather against sex, and a society that would not dream of looking to the Church for guidance about sexual ethics because it sees Christians as being closed and negative about the subject.

In the Song of Solomon, we see a beautiful harmony between love and sex. Sex is the natural expression of a love that has become strong and passionate. It is not hurried; it is anticipated with great delight. Waiting for the consummation of love gives time for preparation and delightful imaginings. Sex is presented as the foundation value of a lasting relationship: boy and girl fall in love and little by little that love grows until it becomes safer to share more intimately. The intimacy of sex comes after marriage, because that is the truly safe place where two people can be vulnerable together, when the commitment of love will be strong enough. Nowadays, we can watch many TV programmes and films, and we are led to believe that sex is the first thing that happens in a relationship, and therefore it is largely recreational rather than meaningful. Love may or may not come after sex. Therein lies much confusion.

Few would argue that we live in a sex-obsessed world in the West, but what fuels this obsession? Is it simply the unbridled lust of a fallen world? Is it the consumerist mantra: have what you want now and pay for it later? I wonder whether it is actually deeper than that. There's something about our busy, noisy, consumerist, commercial world that has evoked a widespread longing for intimacy. Everyone assumes that this is a longing for human intimacy, and most people think the way to get that is through sex. But is there a deeper longing in the souls of those who live in our post-Christendom world? Is there in fact an instinctive longing for divine love? Is the obsession with sex simply the only way people know to respond to the instinct within them that is really linked with loving God?

If this is the case, then maybe those who liked to allegorize the Song of Solomon weren't so far off the mark. There is a connection between sexual love and divine love. It's as though we lack the means of understanding all this properly, but I think that somewhere, wrapped up in the beautiful love poetry, lie some clues about the relationship of intimate human love and intimate divine love. Maybe if we could push past all the embarrassment, innuendo, misunderstanding and the rest, we could find a way of helping people discover that the yearnings within them are actually yearnings for the divine—not a disapproving, sex-disliking, rule-making God, but a passionate, holy God who is full of that love which many waters cannot quench.

Maybe if more in the Church could listen at a deeper level to our young people, there would be fewer judgmental frowns towards sexual licentiousness, and more recognition that they are expressing a deep longing for divine love. It might affect how we relate to and pray for them.

Reflection

How do you feel about having the Song of Solomon in the Bible? Try reading it all the way through. Why do you think our society is so obsessed with sex? What are the deeper longings you hear in this?

Prayer

Take my love; my Lord I pour
at thy feet its treasure-store;
take myself, and I will be
ever, only, all for thee.

FROM THE HYMN 'TAKE MY LIFE AND LET IT BE'

BY FRANCES HAVERGAL (1836–79)

Grumbling against God

From Mount Hor they set out by the way to the Red Sea, to go around the land of Edom; but the people became impatient on the way. The people spoke against God and against Moses, 'Why have you brought us up out of Egypt to die in the wilderness? For there is no food and no water, and we detest this miserable food.' Then the Lord sent poisonous serpents among the people, and they bit the people, so that many Israelites died. The people came to Moses and said, 'We have sinned by speaking against the Lord and against you; pray to the Lord to take away the serpents from us.' So Moses prayed for the people. And the Lord said to Moses, 'Make a poisonous serpent, and set it on a pole; and everyone who is bitten shall look at it and live.' So Moses made a serpent of bronze, and put it upon a pole; and whenever a serpent bit someone, that person would look at the serpent of bronze and live.

NUMBERS 21:4–9

I sometimes think we live in a society that is passionate about grumbling. Watch some TV programmes and you get the impression that there is nothing that entertains us more than finding something we can have a really good moan about. It may be the neighbours from hell, holidays from hell or nightmare builders (to name but a few)—whatever it is, it perversely improves the feel-good factor if we can find someone who can be the guilty party, the object of our complaint. I'm not sure what it says about human nature, but one thing is for sure, it's nothing new. Moses knew all about people complaining!

The book of Numbers is the fourth book of the Bible, and it tells us the story of Israel's journey from Mount Sinai to the plains of

Moab on the border of Canaan. There are a number of stories in the book that are to do with the people of Israel complaining against God and Moses. In today's reading, we find the people of Israel becoming tired and hungry on their wilderness wanderings. Although God has provided manna from heaven for them (Exodus 16:31), they have become bored with it and are starting to long for other food. They go to Moses and say, 'Moses, why have you dragged us out of Egypt on this long journey into this miserable desert where we will surely die? There's no bread, precious little water, and we detest this miserable manna that we have to endure every day.' We don't hear Moses' response, which might be just as well! It really can't have been easy for these folks. It's no fun journeying through the desert with enemies threatening you at every turn, and it's not surprising that they had their bad days. They do what many of us do when facing a difficult time: they start to idealize the past. 'Why bring us out of Egypt?' they say, as if Egypt was a bed of roses. They have forgotten just how terrible life was for them back there. They have forgotten how deeply they pleaded with God to deliver them. They have forgotten what it was like to live as slaves.

We don't know what Moses' response is to these complaints, but we do know that the Lord is not impressed. His response is to send venomous snakes, which come into the Israelite camp and bite many people, a number of whom die. It seems a drastic response from God, but the fact is that his people have got stuck in a mentality of complaint, and it is as though God has to speak through a megaphone before they will hear. Their complaint about the manna is serious. The gift of manna was an expression of God's grace—it was his provision for his people during a time of trial. But once the people start to allow themselves to complain, their souls become poisoned and they reject the very thing that God has given to sustain them. They have become so deaf to God that he has to use shock tactics, and it works. They come to their senses, ask for God's forgiveness and are delivered from the snakes. Once they have become humble, God is able to provide a means of healing.

When life becomes difficult for us, it is very natural to want to find expression for our hurt. Most of us have known times when we have looked to heaven and conveyed a message to God along the lines of 'can't you do better than this?' These moments can actually be the starting-point of renewal. We can be in a situation where we feel hurt or rejected in some way and where we want to hit out at someone, particularly the one who is responsible for the difficulties we are in. We cannot avoid the feelings aroused in us when we are hurt, but we do have choice about how we respond. The children of Israel decided to go down the blame road. They blamed God for sending them boring food, and they blamed Moses for taking them out of Egypt. By doing so, the gift of grace that God was giving them started to taste sour in their mouths, and they developed a fantasy about the past.

Churches can go through wilderness times. The worship can feel dull, the preaching dry; we get irritated by members of the congregation and become judges of all that the church is failing to do well. Our perceptions may be right: the worship may really need to improve; the preacher may need new sources of inspiration; relationships may be poor in the congregation, and the church may be failing in its outreach. But it is what we do with these feelings that counts. Do we settle into a grumbling mode and start to invent an idealized past, or do we take our feelings to God? If we develop a habit of complaining, then even the good things that God gives us will start to taste bitter. The alternative to complaint is intercession —taking our concerns about our church and crying out to God in a longing for renewal. It is then time for us to listen, and God may show us, or others, practical ways for bringing new life to our church.

Reflection

As you think about your life today, are there things that cause you to complain? What is your way of dealing with them? Is there an equivalent 'manna' for you—something good that God has given you, which you have taken for granted? How could it sustain you today?

Prayer

Lord, thank you that you are not put off by my complaints, and that you look with compassion on me when I am hurting. Help me to turn my complaints into prayer and a longing for your healing and renewal.

Stirred to Hatred

Do to them as you did to Midian, as to Sisera and Jabin at the Wadi Kishon, who were destroyed at En-dor, who became dung for the ground. Make their nobles like Oreb and Zeeb, all their princes like Zebah and Zalmunna, who said, 'Let us take the pastures of God for our own possession.'

O my God, make them like whirling dust, like chaff before the wind. As fire consumes the forest, as the flame sets the mountains ablaze, so pursue them with your tempest and terrify them with your hurricane. Fill their faces with shame, so that they may seek your name, O Lord.

PSALM 83:9–16

I have been very fortunate in my life. I have never had cause to hate anyone. I have lived in peacetime Britain, and no one has ever threatened my family, my homeland or me. I cannot imagine what it must be like to live in the shadow of a very real menace from an enemy. The writer of today's psalm knows about this, however. It is a psalm written in an anger provoked by the threats of enemies.

In verses 5–8, the writer identifies the enemies as Edom, the Ishmaelites, Moab and the Hagrites, Gebal, Ammon, Amalek, Philistia, the people of Tyre and Assyria. These may be unfamiliar names to us, but to the writer they were well known as peoples and nations who could cause great harm to Israel. The response of the psalmist is to urge God to deal violently with them. He recalls the experience of Midian, and many others, and takes heart from the fact that God has punished his enemies before, and therefore can again. The story of the wholesale destruction of Midian is told in Numbers 31:1–11, and it is this kind of event that is recalled now. The psalmist calls upon God to bring windstorms, forest fires and tempests to drive away the enemy.

This is one of several psalms where the writer is quite unrestrained in declaring his passionate hatred of his enemy. There is no question of peace talks or reconciliation; nothing less than the humiliating defeat of the enemy is required. Such psalms sit rather uncomfortably with Jesus' command to 'love your enemies and pray for those who persecute you' (Matthew 5:44). It can actually feel quite confusing for Christians to have such apparently contradictory approaches in the Bible. For two millennia, Christian theologians have tried to work out exactly what Jesus meant by that command to love the enemy, and we know that opinions continue to differ, with some defending violent action, and others taking a pacifist route. I'm taking the coward's way out today, and not entering into this debate! What I note is that it is a regular part of human experience that we encounter an enemy, and when we do it is our instinct to hate that enemy and wish for their demise.

Hatred has ruined many lives, because people won't move on from their hatred. Nevertheless, there have been some wonderful examples of people who moved from hatred to forgiveness. John Plummer, now a Methodist pastor, was an American helicopter pilot in the Vietnam War, and he helped organize a napalm raid on the village of Trang Bang in 1972. This bombing is remembered by one terrible photograph, showing a naked girl fleeing in terror from her burning village. For the next 24 years, John was haunted by this picture, knowing that he was one of those who had perpetrated this suffering. He imagined that this little girl, now grown into a woman, must harbour great depths of hatred to him and the others who had killed two members of her family, inflicted serious burns on her, and destroyed her village.

Then, on Veterans Day in 1996, John went to the Vietnam memorial in Washington DC. He came with a group of other pilots, each of whom laboured under a great sense of guilt from the war. He then heard a young Vietnamese woman speak to the gathered crowd. He suddenly realized that the young woman was the very girl from the picture. Her name was Kim, and she told of her suffering and the suffering of her people. She then went on to say: 'If I could talk face to face with the pilot who dropped the bombs, I would tell him we cannot change history, but we should try to do good things for the present and for the future to promote peace.'

John pushed through the crowd to get to her just before she got into a taxi to leave. Weeping with shame, he confessed to being one of the pilots responsible for her pain. The meeting was deeply therapeutic for John as he received Kim's forgiveness. He wrote, 'Kim saw my grief, my pain, my sorrow… She held out her arms to me and embraced me. All I could say was "I'm sorry; I'm sorry"—over and over again. And at the same time she was saying, '"It's all right, I forgive you."' [11] They have since become close friends. Kim could have harboured deep resentment and hatred because of what happened to her and her family, but instead she chose a different way—the way of forgiveness. Terrible things can happen in our lives, and we can be stirred to passionate hatred. But it is reassuring to know that God has also given us an ability to choose a different way—following the example of his Son, to choose to forgive and let go. In Christ, the passion of hatred can be transformed into the passion of forgiveness, and when this happens it is one of the most wonderful renewals that we can experience.

Reflection

Have you known feelings of hatred? Do you identify with the strength of feeling in the psalm? Spend some moments thinking about Kim's story—what does that say to you today?

Prayer

Lord Jesus, you were tried unjustly, cruelly treated and nailed to a cross for no crime whatsoever. Despite your terrible pain, you turned from hatred to forgiveness and opened a new way for peace in your world. Whenever I am tempted to dislike and even hate, help me to follow your example, to forgive freely and live at peace with all people.

Grieving Anger

[Jesus said,] 'You snakes, you brood of vipers! How can you escape being sentenced to hell? Therefore I send you prophets, sages, and scribes, some of whom you will kill and crucify, and some you will flog in your synagogues and pursue from town to town, so that upon you may come all the righteous blood shed on earth, from the blood of righteous Abel to the blood of Zechariah son of Barachiah, whom you murdered between the sanctuary and the altar. Truly I tell you, all this will come upon this generation.

'Jerusalem, Jerusalem, the city that kills the prophets and stones those who are sent to it! How often have I desired to gather your children together as a hen gathers her brood under her wings, and you were not willing! See, your house is left to you, desolate. For I tell you, you will not see me again until you say, "Blessed is the one who comes in the name of the Lord."'

MATTHEW 23:33–39

If you ever doubted that Jesus was a man of strong passions, then you need look no further than this passage. In the previous chapter, Jesus has issued the greatest commandments—to love the Lord God with all our heart and to love our neighbour as ourselves. These commandments throw into sharp relief the utter hypocrisy of the Pharisees, and they know it. They are furious that Jesus so often outsmarts them and exposes the shallowness of their lives and the corruption of their ways. They have got the people where they want them, and they enjoy their power and influence. Jesus is a threat to their position, and so they nag away at him day and night. While Jesus is usually calm and measured in his response to them, on the occasion of today's reading you get the impression that something snaps and he really lets rip. The verses above come at the end of that fearful passage where he castigates the scribes and Pharisees seven times. He fumes with uninhibited rage against them, and lists their crimes. He calls them poisonous snakes; he threatens them with hell; he accuses them of murder. If we had been with him at this time, we would probably have felt very uncomfortable. Did Peter say to John, 'He's really lost it this time,' and wonder anxiously what this would provoke?

The second part of this passage tells us something about what was driving Jesus' anger. It isn't just that he has been provoked once too often by the Pharisees and thus finally loses his temper. At the end of his woes and his judgments, he weeps over Jerusalem, and it is not a weeping of hatred; it is a weeping of loss. Surprisingly, he suddenly uses the image of motherhood: 'O Jerusalem, I wanted so much to gather you together, as a mother hen gathers her chicks.' It is an astonishing leap from aggressive fury to tender care, but it is a leap that every parent knows. One moment you are fuming at some bit of defiant behaviour, and the next you are filled with compassion as you see your child's vulnerability. It is clear that Jesus' anger is motivated by nothing other than passionate love for a lost and scattered people.

We find several expressions of rage in the pages of the Bible, and while I don't think this can ever be used to justify violent actions, I do think it is recognition that there are times in our lives when we can feel deep stirrings of anger. Small children don't worry about whether it is right or wrong to show emotion and it is only slowly that we develop skills to control our feelings. In some cases, these skills are not learned well, and anger erupts in adulthood and brings much harm. In other cases, too much control is learned and there is no safe place for anger to be expressed, so it becomes internalized and can cause depression. Few of us have it perfectly right, but most of us have developed systems that more or less work. It seems to me that passages like today's show us that God understands the depth of feelings within us. I am sure he does not excuse irresponsible expressions of anger that damage others, but I do think he *understands* what it is that drives us to anger, and is concerned that we find safe places for that emotion.

Some anger does bring about remarkable renewal. One of the reasons why Gandhi became a great leader was because he was so angered by the injustices he witnessed in South Africa when he worked there as a young man. He frequently felt angered by injustice, yet never used that anger to justify violence against others. Sometimes we feel we must be so 'Christian' that we should constantly be measured and calm; however, by doing so, we may be missing a route of renewal. Jim Cotter has written some very moving contemporary paraphrases of the psalms. His version of Psalm 39 is fascinating. This is a psalm in which the writer wrestles with strong feelings of anger. Jim Cotter's version includes these lines:

> *Possessed by the demon of anger*
> *swept along by the vortex of rage*
> *I was an easy target for the powerful*
> *a well-aimed blow and I fell*

> *Yet I need the fire in my belly*
> *its heat and its light to move me*
> *I need it to spur me to action*
> *rage become love in the service of others.*[12]

This describes so well the internal conflict of managing overwhelming feelings of anger. Such feelings make us very vulnerable, yet the 'fire in our belly' can be the stimulus that causes us to bring about changes for justice and peace. By the transforming grace of God and following the example of Jesus, we need rage to become love in the service of others. Many have known the renewing work of the Spirit of God in their lives when their anger at some injustice moves them into a field of service where they become agents of God's healing love.

❖

Reflection

What makes you angry? Can you find ways of expressing it to God? What fire 'burns in your belly'? Can you think of ways in which it can be turned into love in the service of others?

Prayer

Try writing a few lines of a psalm to express how you feel either about something that is personally threatening you, or about an injustice that you feel strongly about.

Friday

Love for Christ

Yet whatever gains I had, these I have come to regard as loss because of Christ. More than that, I regard everything as loss because of the surpassing value of knowing Christ Jesus my Lord. For his sake I have suffered the loss of all things, and I regard them as rubbish, in order that I may gain Christ and be found in him, not having a righteousness of my own that comes from the law, but one that comes through faith in Christ, the righteousness from God based on faith. I want to know Christ and the power of his resurrection and the sharing of his sufferings by becoming like him in his death, if somehow I may attain the resurrection from the dead.

PHILIPPIANS 3:7–11

Paul begins chapter 3 of his letter to the Philippians with the word 'Finally'. In fact, he is only about halfway through the letter! I rather like Paul's 'finally's—it's as though he has a final thought which then makes contact with one of his enthusiasms, so he just has to keep on writing about it. The 'finally' of today's passage is to do with rejoicing in the Lord. Paul finds many things to rejoice in the Lord about, and I imagine he would never have been found very far from joy. Having encouraged the believer in the first verse to rejoice, he then issues a warning in verse 2 to 'beware of the dogs', a common term of abuse in the Bible, in this instance applied to those who are trying to make Christianity a religion of works rather than grace—in other words, saying that the way to earn favour with God is to work for it, impressing him with many righteous actions.

Paul goes on to say that if Christianity really were that kind of religion, then he would be doing rather well. He was circumcised on the eighth day, which was exactly the right time; he was from the tribe of Benjamin, which was viewed as a very fine tribe; he was a true-blooded Jew, who had the finest Jewish education from Gamaliel (Acts 22:3); he was a Pharisee, so he knew and obeyed all the rules, and what's more he was extremely zealous and not so long ago he was giving his life to persecuting the Christians. Any pious Jew would have been extremely impressed by these credentials and would assume that God would also be greatly impressed. When Paul met Jesus, however, all that changed.

Today's passage makes it clear that once he met Christ, he realized that all those carefully listed advantages were worth absolutely nothing. This was quite something for Paul, who had put so much store by these things before his conversion. But he has now met Christ, and knowledge of him is infinitely more valuable than the rule-keeping, human-impressing religion that once drove him. For the sake of Christ, he has given up all of this and now regards it as 'rubbish' (v. 8). The Greek word is *skubala*, which literally means 'excrement'. In other words, he is none too impressed with it! Paul is so aware of the vast change that has taken place in his life; he knows that it is all due to his personal encounter with Jesus Christ on the Damascus road. From that moment, he has grown to know Jesus better and better: he is the reason that Paul lives and breathes; he is the source of his joy and the foundation of his hope; he is his life's passion. Thus, he goes on to write that his great longing is to 'know Christ'. Yes, he has met him, but he wants to really *know* him, and that Greek word *ginoskein* is a strong word that refers to personal knowledge, not just academic knowledge. In the Greek translation of the Old Testament, it is used to translate *yada*, a word that is used on occasions for sexual intercourse (for example, 'Adam knew Eve, and she conceived and bore Cain'—Genesis 4:1). It is a knowledge that brings about unity between the two who know each other. Accordingly, Paul does not use this word lightly.

His passion is to know Jesus fully, and he understands that this means he has to become acquainted with both the powerful resurrected life in Jesus, and also the sorrowing crucified life of

Jesus. This is a dangerous knowledge, for to be drawn into the sufferings of Christ is no light thing. The prophecies about the Messiah in the Old Testament, and the stories of Jesus in the New Testament, make very clear just how deeply our Lord suffered. It is very tempting to want to know Jesus at arm's length—to know him in a way that is useful to us, but no further. Paul models for us the true life of the disciple, which is to draw so close to Jesus that we begin to feel as he does. As we engage in his hurting, wounded world, so we feel his grieving; when we encounter Pharisaism, we feel his anger and his weeping over Jerusalem; when we publicly follow him, we risk persecution, even following his example of giving his life. At the same time, knowing Jesus means being drawn into his resurrection life. It means knowing the miracle of healing when we encounter sickness, the miracle of salvation when we meet the lost, and the miracle of deliverance when we meet the oppressed.

In the book of Revelation, it is the church of Ephesus which is criticized by Jesus for having lost its first love (Revelation 2:4). Many renewals begin when we become aware that our love for God has gone cold, and our faith has subsequently lost its vitality. John Wesley's personal renewal began when his heart was 'strangely warmed' at a prayer meeting. Such experiences are not ones that we can arrange or manufacture, but we can take moments to remind ourselves of the Lord whom we serve, and we can develop a longing in our heart to know him more deeply.

Reflection

How well do you feel you know Jesus? What do you think you would need to do to get to know him better? Spend a few moments asking him to warm your heart and renew your love for him.

Prayer

O love divine, how sweet thou art!
When shall I find my longing heart
all taken up by thee?
I thirst, I faint and die to prove
the greatness of redeeming love,
the love of Christ to me.

CHARLES WESLEY (1707–88)

Yearning for Righteousness

Come now, you rich people, weep and wail for the miseries that are coming to you. Your riches have rotted, and your clothes are moth-eaten. Your gold and silver have rusted, and their rust will be evidence against you, and it will eat your flesh like fire. You have laid up treasure for the last days. Listen! The wages of the labourers who mowed your fields, which you kept back by fraud, cry out, and the cries of the harvesters have reached the ears of the Lord of hosts. You have lived on the earth in luxury and in pleasure; you have fattened your hearts on a day of slaughter. You have condemned and murdered the righteous one, who does not resist you.

JAMES 5:1–6

The letter of James is traditionally regarded as being written by James the brother of Jesus, a significant leader in the early Church (see Acts 15). We can't be certain about this, and the writer simply calls himself 'James, a servant of God' (James 1:1). It is a letter that has not always been popular in the Church. Luther called it an 'epistle full of straw, because it contains nothing evangelical'. He felt there was too much emphasis on works rather than faith.

The letter certainly covers a wide area of Christian behaviour, and it emphasizes that Christian commitment must relate to every area of life, and faith must be expressed through works, otherwise it is quite impractical. There is no point in hearing the word if we don't do what it says (James 1:23). It is also a letter with a great strength of feeling for social justice. William Barclay writes of James' letter, 'Not even the most cursory reader of the Bible can fail to be impressed with the social passion which blazes through its pages.

No book condemns dishonest and selfish wealth with such searing passion as it does.'[13]

Our passage for today is a section from the letter in which James makes a scathing attack on the rich. He is speaking to those who feel that they can live in safety. They have made their money; they have their house; they have security for the future and so they can live at one step removed from those who cannot enjoy such wealth and ease. The second part of this passage reveals that the reason why James is particularly angry with this group is because they have made their money through unjust means. They have not paid their labourers a fair wage, and have defrauded them. These labourers have cried out to God in their suffering, and he has heard them, and is planning acts of justice and punishment towards those who have made these innocent ones suffer. James lives close to God, and you get the impression that he has prophetically listened in to these cries for help addressed to heaven, and he has felt God's compassionate and righteous response.

Reading a passage like this can easily drive us straight into guilt. Most of us who live in the Western world live in great luxury compared to those in the developing world, who have a daily battle with poverty. Not only is there a terribly unjust distribution of wealth across the world, but the way we use our wealth in the West often increases the suffering of our developing-world neighbours. In recent years, we have witnessed a number of exposés of clothing producers who have been manufacturing their garments in developing-world countries and paying their workers a pittance of a wage. The rich buy more clothes than they need at the expense of fellow humans who work in grim conditions for little pay. I am sure that James would want us to respond with penitence to this, but he would want more than just a sense of guilt. He would want deeds rather than words. We Christians in the West can get 'guilt fatigue' when we think of the poor elsewhere. To feel guilt of this sort too often can drain us of life, energy and vision. This is not what James wants. He wants God's people to be stirred with passion to *do* something, to use their wealth to relieve suffering rather than shore up personal security.

I receive the quarterly bulletin of the International Justice Mission, which gives a brief update of the excellent work they do in parts of the world where the very poor are suffering at the hands of those who are materially stronger than they are. In the Winter 2004 report, Gary Haugen, president of IJM, writes of his colleagues in the front line of the work:

My IJM colleagues are engaging in the struggle with evil because they believe in something bullies cannot see: the advancing kingdom of God. And because of the assurance of Jesus of Nazareth that 'the gates of hell shall not prevail against it' (Matthew 16:18), they do not grow weary of doing good because they believe an ancient promise from their Maker— that they shall 'reap a harvest if they do not give up' (Galatians 6:9).[14]

He goes on to write about one of his workers, whom he calls Michael. This man was working to release a group of brick kiln slaves in South Asia. The owners of the slaves organized a mob of over a hundred, who attacked Michael and his small team of co-workers. Thankfully they survived, and he wrote, 'It is not me that I stood courageously to face anything, but the Holy Spirit alone who took control of the situation and handled it well and helped us to accomplish His desire. We returned with great victory of 22 released slaves.'

Engaging in acts of compassion and justice in a world that has strayed so far from God's ways is one well-known route of renewal. It is tempting to wait to be renewed before we actually do something, but if we wait in that way we may never get going. Often it is when we launch out in faith to do something, and meet the Holy Spirit when we get there, the Spirit who is only too willing to work in and through us, that we can be led to an experience of radical personal renewal.

❖

Reflection

How do you feel about your wealth (however small or large)? How do you think God feels about your wealth? Spend a few moments listening to him. Is there any way in which the Lord wants to lead you out to bring his justice and freedom into a part of his world?

Prayer

Lord, I look across your world and I am easily overwhelmed by the injustice and suffering that I see. But don't let me settle in guilt and despair; stir me by your Spirit to be an agent of your just and holy ways.

Life (Red)

Introduction

The week before Easter is traditionally known as 'Holy Week'. It begins with the story of the triumphant entry into Jerusalem, and the early days of the week are full of stories of Jesus in the city as the events build up to the Last Supper, the agony in Gethsemane, the trial and crucifixion. By Saturday, we are weary in our grief, and then on Sunday morning we wake up to the news of glorious resurrection. It is a week we know so well, and yet it is not one we want to miss. We need time to journey through this week, following our Lord, getting close to him, listening and pondering and becoming open to the renewing Spirit, who brings the words of scripture to life once again.

We shall be working with Gospel passages this week, and shall focus in particular on the stories of the trial and cross before we reach the glorious news of Easter morning. Red is the colour for this week. Liturgically, it is the colour for saints' days, remembering the blood of the martyrs. It is also the colour for Pentecost and all gifts and ministries of the Spirit, such as healing. It is the colour for this week as we remember the blood of our Saviour poured out for us, as well as the mighty work of the Spirit in raising him to life. The liturgical colour changes on Easter Day to white, and you may like to think of this day as a 'white' day. As you think of the light spectrum, white is what you get when all the colours of the rainbow come together, and Easter does indeed bring together the themes that our colours have been representing during Lent.

At the beginning of this week, you may like to say this prayer:

Father in heaven
this is the week when we journey close to your Son
visiting once again the sacred stories of his suffering and glory.
Send your Holy Spirit to my heart and mind
Open me to new insights
Give me a listening heart
Free me to follow you without fear
Lead me in the pathways of renewal
Amen.

House of Prayer and Praise

Then Jesus entered the temple and drove out all who were selling and buying in the temple, and he overturned the tables of the money-changers and the seats of those who sold doves. He said to them, 'It is written, "My house shall be called a house of prayer"; but you are making it a den of robbers.'

The blind and the lame came to him in the temple, and he cured them. But when the chief priests and the scribes saw the amazing things that he did, and heard the children crying out in the temple, 'Hosanna to the Son of David', they became angry and said to him, 'Do you hear what these are saying?' Jesus said to them, 'Yes; have you never read, "Out of the mouths of infants and nursing babies you have prepared praise for yourself"?'

He left them, went out of the city to Bethany, and spent the night there.

MATTHEW 21:12–17

Jesus has been travelling towards Jerusalem for a while. He alone knows what awaits him when he gets there. The disciples know something's up, but despite Jesus' warnings about what is going to happen, they are still uncertain. When they reach Jerusalem, they are no doubt surprised to find a crowd awaiting them, and even more surprised when they see them hailing Jesus as king, cutting branches from the palm trees and laying them before him as he rides into Jerusalem on the back of a donkey (Matthew 21:7). I imagine that that night the disciples are quite buoyant and perhaps put to the backs of their minds some of Jesus' rather puzzling and gloomy prophecies about arrest and death.

On the next day (Mark 11:12), Jesus decides to go up to the

temple, and there he does something for which I suspect few were prepared. He has a fit of rage and crashes around the Court of the Gentiles, causing a huge disturbance. The temple was for Jews only, apart from one section that was open to Gentiles. They were permitted to gather here and to pray and worship. At festival times, booths were set up for the buying and selling of animals for sacrifices. There were also money-changers, because people had to pay their temple tax in the local currency. By the time Jesus arrived in the temple, there was considerable activity in terms of money-changing, and not only that, but, according to Mark, people were buying things and carrying them through the temple courts (Mark 11:16). The net result of all this was that places which had been set aside for prayer were being used for noisy commercial exchanges and financial gains. Prayer had been sacrificed in the cause of commercialism. It all sounds rather familiar to us, living in the 21st century.

Jesus' response to this is fury, and he prophetically drives out of the temple all those who are defiling it. As this area of the temple is evacuated by the money-changers, who are desperately trying to sweep up their coins, their place is taken by the poor and disabled, who hear that Jesus is around. They couldn't get near earlier, because they had no money to change. They had been pushed out. Now they are being welcomed in, and when they find Jesus, Matthew tells us that he heals them. What an amazing scene this must have been: Jesus standing among the remains of broken booths in a near-empty section of the temple, coins scattered across the floor; then, scrambling over the ruins, this beleaguered group of people coming to find their healing from Jesus.

Another thing that happens on this remarkable day is that the children are somehow or other filled with a spirit of praise. They keep singing 'Hosanna to the Son of David'. I don't imagine that this is a smart little choir with washed faces in neatly ironed choir robes. It sounds like a remarkable, spontaneous eruption of praise, working through the unspoilt spirits of children. It is this last fact that finally causes the Pharisees to snap. These ill-educated, undiscerning children, spiritual nobodies according to the laws of the Pharisees, are daring to proclaim Jesus as the Son of David. They find it appalling that children can be so blasphemous, and they ask Jesus if he can hear it, assuming that if he has any decency about him, he will be as shocked as they are. Jesus angers them even more by his response, which is to quote scripture and remind the Pharisees that God draws praise out of the mouths of children and infants. In so doing, Jesus makes it clear that God is inspiring this, and the shadows of disapproval and disgust darken even further in the souls of the Pharisees.

Recent years have seen many testimonies of churches coming into a renewal of life. Usually at some point in the renewal process powers that have held sway in the church for many years feel threatened. New people come in and threaten old customs. There is often a painful encounter of some kind, and the church either returns to its old ways, or there is a move forward to a more spiritual, prayerful life, where the poor, those unfamiliar with church customs, the sick and needy can at last find a place of belonging in the church. Then people can often start to worship with the spontaneous enthusiasm of children, but there's usually a group of disapproving people not too far away, ready to decry such behaviour. Today's story encourages us to follow Jesus in the way of renewal, but to acknowledge that it is not a way that is without cost and pain.

Reflection

If you belong to a church, think about its life. What is the story of renewal in this church? If Jesus visited today, would he need to turn over tables to make space for the needy? How easy is it for people to worship there with the freedom of children?

Prayer

Table-turning Jesus, visit my life and create good spaces where I can pray and worship freely; visit the church where I worship. Don't let us be too neat and tidy. May we be a place of welcome and healing, where children of all ages can sing their hosannas with freedom.

The Agony in the Garden

He came out and went, as was his custom, to the Mount of Olives; and the disciples followed him. When he reached the place, he said to them, 'Pray that you may not come into the time of trial.' Then he withdrew from them about a stone's throw, knelt down, and prayed, 'Father, if you are willing, remove this cup from me; yet, not my will but yours be done.' Then an angel from heaven appeared to him and gave him strength. In his anguish he prayed more earnestly, and his sweat became like great drops of blood falling down on the ground. When he got up from prayer, he came to the disciples and found them sleeping because of grief, and he said to them, 'Why are you sleeping? Get up and pray that you may not come into the time of trial.'

LUKE 22:39–46

The week began with Jesus riding triumphantly into Jerusalem and the city reverberating with the praises of children. The following day, Jesus expresses prophetic rage in the temple, which precipitates hostility from the religious leaders. In all the Gospels, you get a sense of the storm clouds gathering as the week progresses. We have now reached the Thursday of that week, and Jesus has just had the Passover meal with his friends; this will become the pattern for our holy communion. After this fellowship meal, he leads his disciples to a favourite place of prayer, the Garden of Gethsemane, which is on the Mount of Olives. Jesus knows he is only hours away from the immense ordeal ahead of him. He urges his disciples to pray as he longs that they may not have to 'come into the time of trial'.

Then he withdraws from his disciples, kneels on the ground and begins to pray. It is a time of great testing for Jesus. Before his public ministry began, he experienced a time of testing in the desert. Now he is tested in the garden. The themes of garden and desert are strong in the Bible. Genesis starts with a story set in a garden from which humans are eventually exiled. We have seen that the desert is also a common theme in the Bible, contrasting with the image of the fertile garden in the early verses of Genesis. But the garden of Genesis is also a place of great temptation, and here is Jesus, back in the garden, like the first Adam in the Garden of Eden—and, like Adam, he is also greatly tempted by Satan. Whereas the first Adam fails and loses his garden, Jesus wins this battle and soon will win for his people the most wonderful garden of paradise (which means 'exquisite garden').

In these moments of prayer, Jesus engages in a most intense battle. In the desert, before his ministry began, Jesus was tempted by Satan to avoid the costly side to his ministry and to use his divine powers for his own good. Now Jesus is being tempted again. How he longs for his Father to come up with another plan, offer an escape route—anything that would mean he could avoid the cross. He even asks his Father this, so secure is he in his love that he knows he won't shock him by asking. Just as he feels he might be floundering, an angel from heaven appears and gives him strength. What an amazing task for that angel, to be called by the Father and given the instruction, 'Go and strengthen my Son', and then to draw near to the Son of God at this time of great testing. I wonder how the angel strengthens Jesus. Is it one of the angels who ministered to Jesus in the desert (Matthew 4:11)? Perhaps he reminds Jesus of those words that the Father publicly proclaimed at his baptism, 'You are my Son, the Beloved' (Luke 3:22). However it happens, Jesus is strengthened, but he still feels the intensity of the situation, as he literally sweats blood.

Jesus not only has the company of an angel in this garden, but he also has his friends. As he goes to them for support, however, he finds that they are asleep. Luke tells us that they are sleeping because of grief. As they observe their Lord praying with such passionate intensity they cannot bear it. They know something terrible is going to happen, that Jesus will be taken from them, so they retreat in the way that humans often do when faced with something unbearable—to the safety of the world of sleep, where they can shut out the reality of what is happening. Like the first Adam in the first garden, they hide, and God comes looking for them. They wake up with a start, and Jesus calls them to pray again with the same words, 'Pray that you may not come into the time of trial.' This is quite an insight into the power of prayer: there are times when prayer will spare us from unbearable trials. How many trials do we have to endure because we have failed to pray earlier on?

There are times in the Christian life when we do find ourselves being taken into Gethsemane places. Maybe, like Jesus, we are at a time where we are facing very hard decisions; the journey ahead looks so frightening, and we feel so weak. We long for there to be another way. We feel vulnerable and afraid, unsure where to turn. How reassuring it is to know that we serve a God who knows this experience so well, and who sends provisions from heaven to sustain us!

It may be that we feel like the disciples: we dare not draw too close to Jesus, for fear that we may have to share in his sufferings, and so we distance ourselves. And yet to draw close may lead us, and others, deep into his life which is to do with both cross and resurrection. Any renewal will inevitably draw us closer to Jesus, and whether we find ourselves in a garden or a wilderness, we will encounter both his suffering and his glory.

Reflection

Have you known, or do you know at the moment, a Gethsemane time when you are facing a hard trial and you long for things to change? Spend time thinking about this story, and what it says to the desperate situations in which we can find ourselves.

Prayer

Lord Jesus, I am still full of wonder and praise at what you went through in those final hours of your life. Help me to stay alert in my spirit and to pray faithfully.

The Unjust Trial

They took Jesus to the high priest; and all the chief priests, the elders, and the scribes were assembled. Peter had followed him at a distance, right into the courtyard of the high priest; and he was sitting with the guards, warming himself at the fire. Now the chief priests and the whole council were looking for testimony against Jesus to put him to death; but they found none. For many gave false testimony against him, and their testimony did not agree. Some stood up and gave false testimony against him, saying, 'We heard him say, "I will destroy this temple that is made with hands, and in three days I will build another, not made with hands."' But even on this point their testimony did not agree. Then the high priest stood up before them and asked Jesus, 'Have you no answer? What is it that they testify against you?' But he was silent and did not answer. Again the high priest asked him, 'Are you the Messiah, the Son of the Blessed One?' Jesus said, 'I am; and "you will see the Son of Man seated at the right hand of the Power," and "coming with the clouds of heaven."'

MARK 14:53–62

Jesus is arrested and taken to the high priest's house, where he will face a religious trial—the civil trial is to follow. It is night time, and Matthew's account of this story tells us that the Sanhedrin is present. The Sanhedrin was the supreme court of the Jews, composed of scribes, Pharisees, Sadducees and elders of the people. It had 71 members and was presided over by the high priest. It had certain rules: all criminal cases must be tried during the day; criminal cases could not be transacted during Passover; only if the verdict was 'not guilty' could the trial end the same day as it started; the meeting was invalid if it did not meet in its own meeting-place, the Hall of the Hewn Stone in the temple precincts; the evidence for the innocence of the person had to be presented before any evidence for guilt. What is clear, therefore, is that on all these counts, Jesus' trial was totally unjust, and he and all engaged in it would have known this. Such was the hatred of Jesus by these religious leaders that they were willing to break their own sacred rules and customs in order to get rid of him.

The Gospel writers make it very clear that the main task of this trial is to find a watertight reason to put Jesus to death. His persecutors know that if Jesus survives this, he will be a threat that they will not be able to withstand, so they desperately look for witnesses to incriminate him. Eventually, they find a very tenuous charge to do with his apparent pronouncement that he would personally and literally destroy the temple. If it wasn't so tragic, it would be humorous as you wonder how, in the days before explosives, one man could possible destroy such a huge building.

Then the high priest comes in. Of all the religious leaders, he is perhaps the one most concerned about Jesus. His power and influence are under real threat. And so he goes straight for the vital question: 'Are you the Messiah, the Son of the Blessed One?' Jesus had remained silent to the first charge, but now he has to answer as the high priest has put him under oath. This is quite a risk, as if Jesus now answers 'no', the bottom will fall out of the trial and there is no possible charge against him. If he answers 'yes', then Jesus is signing his own death warrant. So, in response to this momentous question, he answers 'yes', and not only that, but he goes further by quoting Daniel 7:13. This answer actually puts the Sanhedrin on trial, for one day at the Great Judgment they will see Jesus again, this time coming in glory on the clouds of heaven, and terrible will be their guilt at this end-time trial.

Outside in the courtyard, another trial is going on. Peter had followed Jesus, and has attempted to listen in on events in the high priest's house. Suddenly, the spotlight turns on him and he too is on trial, interrogated not by important religious leaders, but by ordinary, everyday people, who want to see if he will confess to being a follower. Unlike his master, Peter lies and runs for his life, fulfilling Jesus' sad prophecy about him (Mark 14:30).

Jesus and Peter are both tried at the same time. In Jesus' case, it is an unjust trial perpetrated by people who purport to be the servants of God, yet who have allowed themselves to be corrupted by power; in Peter's case, it is the kind of trial any of us might meet any day, where to answer publicly that we are followers of Jesus could lead to ridicule and, in some countries, a very real threat of persecution and death. Peter's heart is full of fear. He is unprepared. He slept in the garden when he should have been praying. By contrast, Jesus is full of faith. He prayed in the garden, and his soul was prepared. He knows his scriptures, and he knows that although the immediate future is full of pain and injustice, the long-term future is safe, for his Father will one day usher in a just and peaceful world. As we face trials of many kinds, we may so often feel like Peter. We know that Jesus forgave Peter, and so will not condemn us if we repent. But Jesus also urges us to follow his example, and not desperately to justify ourselves or plan swift manoeuvres to avoid pain; he put his trust in his Father's perfect plan, and was therefore at peace.

Reflection

How do you respond when people treat you unjustly at work, or in church? What is your natural response? Is there anything in today's reading that makes you want to change how you respond?

Prayer

My Lord, I marvel at your strength of spirit in the midst of that unjust trial. When I am unfairly judged, help me to lift my eyes above the need to justify myself or punish my accusers, to that scene of the Son of man coming on the clouds of heaven. How I look forward to that day!

In the Palace of Pilate

As soon as it was morning, the chief priests held a consultation with the elders and scribes and the whole council. They bound Jesus, led him away, and handed him over to Pilate. Pilate asked him, 'Are you the King of the Jews?' He answered him, 'You say so.' Then the chief priests accused him of many things. Pilate asked him again, 'Have you no answer? See how many charges they bring against you.' But Jesus made no further reply, so that Pilate was amazed.

MARK 15:1–5

We move from the religious trial to the civil trial. As Peter knows only too well, the cock has crowed and it is early morning (Mark 14:72). The scene is now in Pilate's palace, which was built by Herod the Great just south of the temple area. The Sanhedrin have reached their verdict. Under Roman law they have no power to administer the death sentence, so they must take Jesus to the Roman governor to be tried, and they must let the Roman authorities carry out the punishment.

What kind of a person was Pilate? He was the procurator of the province of Judea, directly responsible to the emperor. It was a very senior post, so he had done well to reach this position. He had been procurator for ten years, and it had been a troubled time. He was completely out of sympathy with the Jews and, in common with most Romans, was contemptuous of the Jewish religion and its customs. The Romans knew the dedication and fervour of the Jewish people, and they resented them for it, and were always nervous of uprisings.

It seems that his dealings with Jesus did not change Pilate, although it may have changed his wife. Some time after the events of this historic Passover, Pilate was called to Samaria to quell an uprising. He met it with quite unnecessary force and violence, and ended up slaughtering many innocent victims. He was ordered to go to Rome to explain himself to the Emperor Tiberius. The emperor, however, died while Pilate was on his way. The fourth century historian Eusebius reported that Pilate committed suicide while on that journey to Rome. Legend has it that wherever Pilate's body was buried, the area was terribly troubled by evil spirits. Eventually, his body was supposedly buried in Switzerland and the mountain Pilatus is named after him.

So, Jesus is facing a man who is clumsy in his dealings with the people and has no natural sympathy for anyone who seems to be leading any kind of uprising. Pilate now takes on his role as the imperial magistrate and the civil trial proceeds. He asks Jesus, 'Are you the King of the Jews?' Unlike his reply to the high priest, Jesus' answer this time is less straightforward. 'You say so.' It is as if he is saying, 'This is what I have been accused of, but you must decide for yourself if I am guilty of this charge and merit the death penalty.' Pilate questions him further, trying to elicit more information, and as in the other Gospel accounts you get the impression that he is trying to help Jesus. He wants Jesus to respond, because if Jesus does not defend himself then, according to Roman law, Pilate would have to pronounce against him there and then. But Mark tells us that Pilate is amazed. He finds Jesus fascinating. Maybe there is something in his spirit that tells him Jesus is more than just a Jewish rebel. Matthew tells us that his wife had a disturbing dream about Jesus, and maybe this is playing on his mind (27:19).

Whatever it is, he provides a way out for Jesus: as this passage goes on to show, he tries the Barabbas plan (Matthew 27:15–18); this seems such a good idea, and one that should surely bring about the release of Jesus. He makes use of a Roman custom, which is to release a prisoner at the Passover festival. Pilate's hope is that the crowd will choose to condemn Barabbas, thereby enabling Jesus to go free. It goes horribly wrong, however, because not only does it not save Jesus, but it releases a dangerous rebel back into the community. Even when Pilate finally sentences Jesus, you get the impression that he is doing so reluctantly, and he literally washes his hands of the whole matter, because something is troubling his conscience. As the action moves on from Pilate, we leave him a troubled man, and we feel that somewhere in his soul he sensed that something terribly, terribly wrong had taken place.

Pilate seems to epitomize the person who is 'nearly there'. He meets Jesus and he senses that there is something different about this man. Pilate may be a man stuck in the groove of his own ways, especially his habit of cruelly repressing the people whose land he and his troops are occupying, and yet for these few moments he has an opportunity to step out of those old ways and live differently. It is as if someone opened a door into a new and better world and invited him to step through, yet his fears prevented him from doing so. We can have moments in our lives when something un-expectedly causes us to see things in a new light, and we have an opportunity to live differently. Such moments may well be occasions when God is calling us into a new way of living, with new attitudes. We become aware of having the choice of living more justly, more lovingly, more as Christ wants us to live. He never forces us, just as Jesus did not force Pilate, but if we do risk taking fresh steps of faith, we can be absolutely sure that Jesus is walking with us, steadying us and excitedly showing us new landscapes and views.

Reflection

Is there any way in which you have got stuck in your thinking about God? What new adventure might Jesus be calling you on?

Prayer

Lord, Pilate had got stuck in his ways and could not see who you were, even when you gave him so many opportunities to see. Help me to open my eyes and my ears to your Spirit, who leads me into all truth.

The Way of Tears

As they led him away, they seized a man, Simon of Cyrene, who was coming from the country, and they laid the cross on him, and made him carry it behind Jesus. A great number of the people followed him, and among them were women who were beating their breasts and wailing for him. But Jesus turned to them and said, 'Daughters of Jerusalem, do not weep for me, but weep for yourselves and for your children. For the days are surely coming when they will say, "Blessed are the barren, and the wombs that never bore, and the breasts that never nursed." Then they will begin to say to the mountains, "Fall on us"; and to the hills, "Cover us." For if they do this when the wood is green, what will happen when it is dry?'

LUKE 23:26–31

We have been following the story of Jesus' unjust trial by the Sanhedrin and the meeting with the curious Pilate, who attempts a deal with the crowd to release him, but finds they prefer Barabbas. Now Jesus is handed over to the Roman soldiers for a duty they have often performed, that of carrying out the most cruel and humiliating means of death that they know. It begins with the 39 lashes and mockery with the crown of thorns, and then involves the slow walk to Golgotha. This was the dreadful custom: the criminal had to walk to the place of crucifixion carrying the cross (or the cross beam). Four soldiers surrounded him, the first of whom would carry a board stating the crime, so that the watching crowd would know exactly why this man was being put to death. This board was then nailed to the cross. They did not take the shortest route, but went round the streets so that as many people as possible could see the fate of those who dared to commit such crimes.

Today's reading takes us to two small scenes on this *via dolorosa*, 'the way of tears'. Luke tells us that the Roman soldiers seize a man called Simon of Cyrene and compel him to carry the cross. Jesus, who is fully human, is so weakened by the beating that he no longer has the strength to carry the cross. The Romans had passed laws forcing anyone to carry a load for them. This was one of their many humiliating ways of signalling that they were the power in the land. So it was that they dragooned Simon to carry this sacred load. Simon was from Cyrene, a leading city in African Libya, and today's Tripoli. He had made a pilgrimage to Jerusalem for the Passover, and had no doubt saved up for a long time to come and celebrate his faith in the holy city. And now he finds himself among a milling crowd, and sees a badly beaten man being forced by soldiers to carry a heavy piece of wood. As Jesus passes him, he stumbles, and maybe it is compassion on Simon's part that causes him to reach out and help him. The next thing he knows is the cold steel of the Roman spear on his shoulder, a sign that he has been chosen to help. He takes the full weight of this desperate load on his shoulders and follows Jesus to the place of crucifixion.

It is very likely that Simon became a Christian after this experience. Mark tells us that he was the father of Alexander and Rufus (Mark 15:21), and he probably mentions this because his readers would have known this family. In Acts 13:1, there is a list of the men of Antioch who sent Paul and Barnabas out on their first great mission to the Gentiles, and the name of one of these is 'Simeon who was called Niger', who, given the reference to 'niger' (meaning 'black') may well be the same Simon. It is quite possible that Simon's walk to Golgotha moved him so much that he became a follower of Jesus. Maybe he stayed around in Jerusalem after Jesus' death and heard the news of the resurrection. Was he the first evangelist to take the good news back to his homeland?

Whatever became of Simon, there is something very poignant about the fact that it was an African who found himself carrying the cross of Christ. No race has suffered such humiliation as the African peoples. Even in the days of the Roman Empire they were being captured and shipped as slaves, and for centuries after that the systematic persecution and enforced slavery of black Africans continued. When Simon carried that cross, it was undoubtedly a prophetic action, unknown to him, but known in the broken heart of God, who saw that these people, more than any other, would feel so deeply the wounds of the cross. But they would also know the joys of resurrection, and it is not without significance that the 20th-century Pentecostal movement began with William Seymour, a poor black man descended from slaves.

The others who are mentioned in this passage are the women. It is typical of Luke to mention them, for he has a heart for those unjustly treated, and women certainly came into that category in first-century Palestine. The women have a special role in this procession to Golgotha. They are the ones who give voice to the gnawing emotion of this event. It was unseemly for men to show grief at funerals, and so the women became the emotional spokespeople, and articulated the grief. These women on the *via dolorosa* are carrying and articulating the horror of the unjust trial and the grief of witnessing Jesus' suffering. Their burden is as heavy as the one placed on Simon's shoulders. Jesus hears their wailing and he pauses for a moment to address them. He tells them not to weep for him, but for themselves and their children, for he knows that the days are not far off when the results of sinfulness and evil will result in the city of Jerusalem being razed to the ground, and, as is so often the case, the women and children will be the innocent sufferers in the wake of human greed and ambition.

It is striking that as God carries his cross on the way to the immense act that will provide a way of healing for his desperately sick world, he notices two groups of people that have suffered so much because of this sickness: black people and women. As you look at the places of suffering throughout the world today, it is so often the black communities that still suffer from prejudice and from severe economic injustice. Across the world, it is still so often the women who are the most vulnerable. There is something deeply comforting about the fact that Jesus noticed such people as he was carrying his cross. He still notices them today, carries them in his heart, and desires that all his followers will also notice them and be fired by the Spirit to do their part in bringing Christ-like healing and justice to bear on their lives.

Reflection

If you are black and/or female, how does this story affect you? If you are white and/or male, how does the story affect you? How do you want to respond?

Prayer

Jesus of the Golgotha road, thank you that you noticed those who were also carrying loads caused by human sinfulness. You allowed them to give to you, and you gave to them. Make me also aware of those who carry such loads, so that I may humbly receive your love through them, and generously share whatever I have.

Grief at Golgotha

Meanwhile, standing near the cross of Jesus were his mother, and his mother's sister, Mary the wife of Clopas, and Mary Magdalene. When Jesus saw his mother and the disciple whom he loved standing beside her, he said to his mother, 'Woman, here is your son.' Then he said to the disciple, 'Here is your mother.' And from that hour the disciple took her into his own home.

After this, when Jesus knew that all was now finished, he said (in order to fulfil the scripture), 'I am thirsty.' A jar full of sour wine was standing there. So they put a sponge full of the wine on a branch of hyssop and held it to his mouth. When Jesus had received the wine, he said, 'It is finished.' Then he bowed his head and gave up his spirit.

JOHN 19:25–30

The sad procession on the *via dolorosa* finally reaches its destination, and it is there that our Lord is nailed to the cross. How poignant for Jesus, who no doubt spent his early years learning carpentry skills from his father; once, he used wood for creative purposes, but now, on wood, his body is put to death. The means of death is deliberately slow, and so we have in our scriptures detailed stories of Jesus in his final hours of life. We know from these stories that he was not alone. There were others crucified alongside him, and we know that he spoke with them (Luke 23:39–43). There were also those who journeyed to the cross with Jesus and stayed with him while he died. John tells us that Mary his mother was there, his aunt, Mary the wife of Clopas and Mary Magdalene. The beloved disciple was also there. It is said that when those millions of young British and German men fell in the battlefields of the First World

War, the most common word heard on their dying lips was: 'Mother'. At the moment of death, it is a natural instinct to want to be comforted by the one who brought us into the world and nurtured us in our earliest days.

It is astonishing that Mary made it this far. Although she had been given information about the unique nature of her Son by angels and prophets, could anything have prepared her for this? How easy it would have been to have turned back on the *via dolorosa*, and how much we would have understood. Amazingly, though, she stayed with her son, and was there as he took his final gasps of agonized breath; she was there when his lifeless body was removed from the cross, an image that is so beautifully and painfully portrayed by Michelangelo in his sculpture, 'Pieta'. John tells us that the 'beloved disciple' was there as well. Despite his initial cowardice in the garden, he crept forward from the shadows and comes to the cross. Jesus sees him there with his grieving mother, and entrusts Mary into the care of John. No doubt in those first hours of mourning they were of great comfort to each other. Maybe Jesus knew that, of all the people there, they were the ones most open to believing the Easter message that they would experience so wonderfully in two days' time. They could stay with the darkness because they were ones who had a capacity to experience great light.

After he performs this final duty of taking care of his mother, Jesus is now ready to relinquish his earthly life. Even though he is pinned to the cross and has been subjected to every humiliation by the religious and political authorities, you get the sense that Jesus is still very much in control. His oneness with the Father gives him a sense of knowing deeper truths than anyone else present. In his last moments, he cries out: 'I am thirsty.' John tells us that there is some wine nearby, and he would have been very aware of the imagery from the night before—the Passover meal, at which Jesus compared the wine to his blood being poured out. Not only that, but John mentions that the wine-soaked sponge was put on the stalk of a hyssop plant, and, for the Jew, this would have had instant associations with the Passover. In Exodus 12:22, on the night of the first

Passover, Moses instructs the people of Israel to slaughter a lamb, dip a bunch of hyssop in the blood and spread it on the lintel and doorposts of their homes. The blood of the lamb protected the people from the destroying angel that flew over Egypt as the final curse on the stubborn Pharaoh. As Jesus took this wine in his final moments of life, it was full of symbolism, for he was *the* Passover Lamb of God; he was now taking away the sins of the world and providing protection for all people who would trust in him, to save them from the destroying effects of Satan. That is why he could say: 'It is finished.' His earthly ministry was completed, and he could offer back his spirit to his Father.

There are so many books about the crucifixion of Christ. There are mighty theological tomes on the subject of atonement and the meaning and significance of the death of Christ on the cross. There are discussions, and arguments and theories and debates that stretch and challenge our minds. There is a multitude of cassettes and CDs by erudite preachers on the subject. There are well-crafted songs and hymns that move us from understanding to worship. There are countless pieces of art; there are many plays, films and musicals that depict Christ's dying. But there is always a part of me that, when we come again to Good Friday, wants to push past all of that to come afresh to that strange, dark hillside and be as one of those bold disciples, daring to come close, yearning to understand, longing for someone to do something to relieve his suffering. As I do so, I imagine I catch a glimpse of those pain-filled eyes as he lifts his head and looks on each of us with forgiving and eternal love. It is only then, in a moment of wonder and adoration, that we begin to understand a little of what this is all about. And even then, we must be content with only a small measure of understanding. One day, it will all make sense. Until then, we huddle with that small group of believers and allow what seeds of faith and love we have to be planted in that Calvary soil.

❖

Reflection

Spend a few moments allowing your mind to imagine the scene. You may like to use these words from Isaac Watts' hymn ('When I survey the wondrous cross') to help you:

> *See from his head, his hands, his feet,*
> *sorrow and love flow mingling down;*
> *did e'er such love and sorrow meet,*
> *or thorns compose so rich a crown?*
> ISAAC WATTS (1674–1748)

Prayer

My Lord, your love is so amazing, so divine. I can scarcely begin to comprehend it, but I believe it and because of it, I offer my soul, my life, my all to you today.

The Dark Cocoon

When it was evening, there came a rich man from Arimathea, named Joseph, who was also a disciple of Jesus. He went to Pilate and asked for the body of Jesus; then Pilate ordered it to be given to him. So Joseph took the body and wrapped it in a clean linen cloth and laid it in his own new tomb, which he had hewn in the rock. He then rolled a great stone to the door of the tomb and went away. Mary Magdalene and the other Mary were there, sitting opposite the tomb.

The next day, that is, after the day of Preparation, the chief priests and the Pharisees gathered before Pilate and said, 'Sir, we remember what that impostor said while he was still alive, "After three days I will rise again."

'Therefore command that the tomb be made secure until the third day; otherwise his disciples may go and steal him away, and tell the people, "He has been raised from the dead", and the last deception would be worse than the first.' Pilate said to them, 'You have a guard of soldiers; go, make it as secure as you can.' So they went with the guard and made the tomb secure by sealing the stone.

MATTHEW 27:57–66

We now move from the dreadful event of the cross to the mournful tale of the tomb. Gone are the great crowds that witnessed the trial, the journey and the death of Jesus. Gone is the drama of the terrible crucifixion. Instead, we have a story to do with the lonely quietness of death. We find ourselves in the company of a rich man from Arimathea and two faithful Marys: Mary Magdalene and Mary the mother of Joses (Mark 15:47). John tells us that Nicodemus was also there (John 19:39). Ironically, we find ourselves again with a Joseph and a Mary, and the language of laying the body in the tomb sounds familiar to us. It is a haunting echo of that beautiful moment when another Joseph and Mary laid their baby in the manger and worshipped him. That Joseph and Mary delighted in the miraculous gift of new life. By sad contrast, this Joseph and Mary are not laying a newborn child in a manger; they are laying into a tomb the lifeless body of a cruelly killed man.

Joseph was clearly a good man. He and Nicodemus must have been a great support and comfort to Jesus. Most of the wealthy and influential had turned their backs on Jesus, and it was a group of powerful men who had helped to engineer his capture and death. But Joseph and Nicodemus were two great exceptions. No one knows what role they played in the early Church. Because they were clearly humble men, they chose no prominence, but I think we can be certain they worked away at their friends and colleagues in those early days following the resurrection, opening the minds of perhaps many to discover the Messiah. There is a well-loved legend that in AD61 Philip sent Joseph from Gaul to evangelize to the English and, according to the story, he and his fellow evangelists came to Glastonbury and were the first to preach the gospel on British soil.

On this Friday evening, however, Joseph's role is far more sombre. He generously offers his family tomb, for he is wealthy enough to have one reserved, and it is as yet unused. Now he is offering it to Jesus, as a sign of his great love for him. According to Jewish law, even a criminal's body could not be left hanging all night, especially if the next day was a Sabbath (Deuteronomy 21:22–23), so the body had to be removed from the cross and laid directly in this tomb. The family and friends of Jesus must have been so grateful for this gift. Without Joseph's offer, the body of Jesus would have suffered the fate of those criminals that had no tomb—callously thrown on the rubbish tip, heaping further humiliation and pain on the family.

For those of us who are familiar with the story, we know there is a happy ending coming on Easter morning, but how much did the disciples know? Jesus had often spoken to them about his being handed over to be crucified and that he would then rise again (Luke 24:6–8), but you get the impression that it was more than they could comprehend. The story in today's passage about Pilate sealing the tomb and setting a guard certainly makes clear that Jesus' teaching about rising on the third day had been registered by some. Pilate's actions were to forestall anyone planning a fake rising from the dead. But despite the fact that there was knowledge of a possibility of resurrection, we don't hear of the disciples gathering at the tomb the next day in joyful expectation of a dazzling event. There is no record of a disciple meeting the risen Jesus and saying, 'Ah, there you are! I knew you were going to rise from the dead!' We have to conclude from this that the disciples had decided that a literal resurrection was not going to happen, and they were setting their minds to adjusting to the terrible loss of their friend and master.

Thus, it is likely that they spent that Saturday in a state of shock, grief and bewilderment. Jerusalem was still full of festival life, but the last thing they wanted to do was to celebrate. Who knows what was going on through their minds that night, or how they spent that strange sabbath day after the crucifixion? Did they meet up, or did they spend time on their own? Did they go to the synagogue to worship, or were they so numb in heart and spirit that they could not face it?

For us, the day is known as Holy Saturday, the day that our Lord rested in the tomb. It is the day of calm between the massive events of Good Friday and Easter Sunday. There are times in our lives when it really feels as if we are living between cross and resurrection. We have witnessed suffering either in our own lives or in the lives of others, and we are in a place of shock, grief and bewilderment. We can hope for our Easter Sunday experience, but it can feel like a long way away. These 'Holy Saturdays' can go on for a long time, so it is comforting to know that we are not alone in this experience. Even the most faith-filled disciples knew something of this, and they came through it. Unbeknown to them the life-giving Spirit was on the move. He was about to visit the tomb, the place that was the focus of their fear, grief and despair, but he needed time, and the disciples needed time to prepare.

How we long for difficult and uncertain times to move on quickly to Easter morning, but sometimes it is on these Holy Saturdays that some of the most profound works of renewal take place in our lives. If we will give space for these times, and not try to hurry them on, we will find ourselves in the right place to hear the news of resurrection when it comes. If the butterfly emerges too soon from its chrysalis, it will not survive. That time spent in the dark cocoon is essential to prepare it for its new world. Holy Saturdays can be like those cocoons—they can be tomb places that provide us with space to grieve the old and prepare ourselves for the new.

Reflection

As you look back on your life, can you recall times when you were in a 'Holy Saturday' place? What kept you going during that time?

Prayer

Lord Jesus, when I find myself in a Holy Saturday, remind me that it is not an unsafe place to be, and open me to the possibility of a coming day of resurrection.

Resurrection (White)

In the last six weeks, we have been on a journey of renewal. In the last two weeks, we have drawn close to the suffering and death of our Lord, and yet even in those valleys of shadows we have found shafts of light. Today, we come to the last reading and we meet the risen Lord. We have considered each colour of the rainbow, and in today's story all the colours meet in the prism of the resurrection and become white light. The colours are not eliminated—they are still there, but they find a place of unity.

The Renewal Begins!

When it was evening on that day, the first day of the week, and the doors of the house where the disciples had met were locked for fear of the Jews, Jesus came and stood among them and said, 'Peace be with you.' After he said this, he showed them his hands and his side. Then the disciples rejoiced when they saw the Lord. Jesus said to them again, 'Peace be with you. As the Father has sent me, so I send you.' When he had said this, he breathed on them and said to them, 'Receive the Holy Spirit.'

JOHN 20:19–22

We join this Easter story in the evening. It has been an extraordinary day. After two long, dark nights, the sabbath being over, the women take the earliest opportunity to go to the tomb. Nothing in the Gospels indicates that they were going there with the express purpose of witnessing the resurrection. They went to put spices on the dead body. If they had nurtured a belief in the resurrection, either they were not expecting it that day, or they were expecting it to happen in a way disconnected from the earthly body. Accordingly, when they find the tomb empty, they don't entertain thoughts of resurrection; they assume that Jesus' body has been stolen, and their grief is now compounded with the mystery of the disappearing body. Mary tells Peter and John, who run to the tomb to see the situation for themselves, and in John 20:8 we get the first indication of belief and understanding that a resurrection has taken place, as John writes of himself that 'he saw and believed'.

It is Mary Magdalene who is the first actually to see the risen Jesus, and after that encounter (John 20:10–18) convinces her that the body of Jesus has in some extraordinary way been transformed into resurrection life, she joins John in the company of new believers. All this has happened in the early morning, and for the rest of the morning and afternoon it seems that they remain in the house, doors locked for fear that the religious leaders may seek to arrest them as followers of Jesus. Who knows how the rumours of resurrection might affect the Pharisees, who had worked so hard to destroy Jesus?

Despite the locked doors and the fear, a visitor arrives. They are in no doubt—it is the Lord who stands among them. He looks like Jesus, sounds like Jesus, and comes with a message of peace. It is really impossible to know how those disciples felt at that moment. It was probably a larger group than the apostles. Was Mary the mother of Jesus there? What about the other women who had been at the cross? Did they all have secret doubts that this was just a symptom of bereavement—the imagining of the loved one returning? Somehow the story does not read like that. Only Thomas doubts, and he was not there. Once he sees the risen Jesus he believes (John 20:28). As far as we can understand, all those disciples, once they have seen, heard, touched, eaten with the risen Jesus, know it is definitely him. He is in a body that is recognizably him, yet it has some interesting properties, such as being able to materialize and dematerialize! None of that seems to bother the disciples. There's no story of anyone asking Jesus about what happens to food when a resurrected body eats it. It is as though the fact of his being raised is so glorious, so momentous, of such significance, that their joy surpasses any detailed questioning. They seem to have got the main message straight away—that Christ is risen, death is defeated, Satan is conquered and there is hope for the world. It is as simple and wonderful as that.

In this upper room, as the disciples share in this delight of faith, Jesus then does one very special thing: he breathes on them the Holy Spirit. Renewal and resurrection are inseparable. Because Jesus is raised, we can be renewed. The resurrection was a Trinitarian act: the Son was raised by the will of the Father and by the activity of the Holy Spirit. Paul, writing about this in his letter to the Romans, puts it this way: 'If the Spirit of him who raised Jesus from the dead dwells in you, he who raised Christ from the dead will give life to your mortal bodies also through his Spirit that dwells in you' (Romans 8:11).

When Jesus breathed his Holy Spirit onto his disciples, it was the same Spirit who invaded that tomb of death and transformed the mortal body of Jesus. It is the same Spirit who is available to every believer who puts their trust in the risen Jesus. No tomb is beyond the reach of this remarkable and wonderful Holy Spirit. Nothing is too mortal or earthly for him. Renewal is engaging in what Paul calls 'new life of the Spirit' (Romans 7:6). This is the wonderful gift of the risen Jesus to us.

We have travelled through 46 days of Lent, which brings us to this extraordinary event of Easter. We have been working with the theme of the rainbow of renewal, the multi-coloured activity of the Holy Spirit who brings to earth the things of God. In recent years, that well-known rainbow song from *The Wizard of Oz* has been given new life by Eva Cassidy's much-acclaimed version. I remember once playing this as part of a Christian meditation on hope, and remember so clearly the effect those simple words had on us all:

> *Somewhere over the rainbow, skies are blue*
> *and the dreams that you dare to dream really do come true.*

We paused and instinctively looked up, some with eyes closed, imagining that rainbow, seeing the skies of blue, and making contact with the dreams we once dared to dream, and you could almost feel the hope rising as we engaged in that simple image.

I saw a rainbow again yesterday. I was coming into London on the train to St Pancras Station, which at the time of writing is being rebuilt. The rainbow was shining brilliantly against a thundery dark sky, and beneath it lay a mixture of old ruins and new buildings. I was on my way to a conference hosted by the Archbishop of Canterbury on 'Fresh Expressions', a term used to describe the multitude of new forms of church life that are bubbling up all over the land. It was a wonderfully optimistic conference as we heard stories of those who had dared to believe that their dreams really could come true.

The rainbow of renewal is full of promise for those who are prepared to dream and be adventurous. The rainbow arches over every part of our lives—our broken and wasteland places, and our scenes of rebuilding and new life. It is a rainbow that beckons us, dares us to dream and imagine. It acknowledges the Good Friday hurts; it is prepared to spend however much time is needed in the chrysalis of Holy Saturday; it waits with eager expectation at the bursting forth of new life on Easter Day. May the Holy Spirit bring about this rainbow renewal in our lives.

Reflection

You have reached the end of these daily readings. How do you feel as you reach this point? What have been the main learning points? Where did God touch your life most? Where have you felt renewed? Where do you still long for renewal?

Prayer

Renewing, rainbow Spirit, visit me today and every day. I don't ask you to solve every problem, cure every sickness or answer every question. I ask that you draw me near to the crucified and risen Jesus, so that my life may be one that glorifies the Father and brings your healing life to the places where I live and serve.

Notes

1   *The Way of Renewal*, edited by Michael Mitton, CHP 1998.
2   Gerald Arbuckle, *Grieving for Change*, Geoffrey Chapman 1991, p. 1.
3   'Heaven' by Adrian Plass, published in *City of Gold*, Solway 1997, p. 42.
4   *Youth Praise*, CPAS 1966.
5   T.S. Eliot, *Murder in the Cathedral*, Faber & Faber, second edition 1936, p. 54.
6   'God's Grandeur' by Gerard Manley Hopkins, *Poems and Prose*, Penguin 1953, p. 27.
7   *Carmina Gadelica*, ed. Alexander Carmichael, Floris Books 1992, p. 109.
8   The films are produced by The Sentinel Group, distributed by Gateway Christian Media Ltd, PO Box 11905, London NW10 4ZQ. Tel. 0870 011 8184. Email: orders@gatewaymedia.org.uk
9   Dietrich Bonhoeffer, *The Cost of Discipleship*, SCM 1959, p. 79 (I have used inclusive language).
10 C.S. Lewis, *Surprised by Joy*, Collins Fontana Books 1959, p. 182.
11 *The Lost Art of Forgiving*, Johann Christoph Arnold, Plough 1998. The story can also be found in the October 1997 edition of *Guideposts* magazine.
12 *Through Desert Places*, Jim Cotter, Cairns Publications 1989, p. 85.
13 *The Letters of James and Peter*, William Barclay, St Andrew's Press 1976, p. 116.
14 International Justice Mission, PO Box 58147, Washington DC 20037-8147. www.ijm.org